WOULD YOU BELIEVE …

THE HELSINKI ACCORDS CHANGED THE WORLD?

ALSO BY PETER L.W. OSNOS

An Especially Good View: Watching History Happen

George Soros: A Life in Full (editor)

WOULD YOU BELIEVE ...

BELIEVE ...

THE HELSINKI ACCORDS CHANGED THE WORLD?

Advancing Global Human Rights and, for Decades, Security in Europe

PETER L.W. OSNOS

with HOLLY CARTNER
Former Executive Director of Helsinki Watch

PLATFORM

New York

Peter Osnos, Publisher
Platform Books
900 West End Avenue Ste 16A
New York, NY 10025

Christine E. Marra, Managing Editor

Book design by Jane Raese
Set in 12.5 point Adobe Caslon

Editorial production by *Marra*thon Production Services,
www.marrathoneditorial.net

Cataloging-in-Publication data for this book is available from the
Library of Congress.

ISBN 978-1-7359968-9-9 (HC)

Printed in the United States of America
First Edition: May 2021
10 9 8 7 6 5 4 3 2 1

To the memory of
Ambassador Albert W. Sherer Jr. and Carroll Russell Sherer,
whose efforts on behalf of the Helsinki Accords
and so much else in their lives of service were formidable.

And to all those whose commitment to human rights
came with great risks and ultimately, but not always,
the results they worked to achieve.

Contents

Prologue

IT HAS BEEN fifty years since diplomats from thirty-three
European nations, plus the United States and Canada,
first convened in Geneva and Helsinki for the purpose of
devising, at long last, the post–World War II political, economic, and social structure for the continent. Europe had
been bedeviled by territorial and ideological conflicts in the
twentieth century; the devastation had been vast and borders
rearranged by the ambitions of dictators, imperialists, and
their generals.

In what was called the Helsinki Final Act or the Helsinki
Accords, the thirty-five signatories at a summit meeting that
ran from July 30 to August 1, 1975, agreed to the following
principles, known as the Decalogue:

Sovereign equality, respect for the rights inherent in
    sovereignty.
Refraining from the threat or use of force.
Inviolability of frontiers.
Territorial integrity of states.
Peaceful settlement of disputes.
Non-interference in internal affairs.
Respect for human rights and fundamental freedoms,
    including the freedom of thought, conscience,
    religion, or belief.

Equal rights and self-determination of peoples.
Cooperation among states.
Fulfillment in good faith of obligations under
    international law.

Measuring history in eras, the Helsinki Accords defined
a period of what in retrospect seems relative stability in Europe and among the allies and adversaries around the world.
The accords marked the high point of what was known as
détente, the years in the 1970s when the superpowers—the
United States and the Soviet Union—pursued agreements to
ease security tensions and increase commerce and contacts.
In the presidencies of Richard Nixon and Gerald Ford, that
policy prevailed against those who believed that dealing with
the Kremlin would inevitably end in disaster.

Détente ended, definitively, with the Soviet invasion of
Afghanistan on December 24, 1979. This military incursion in
South Asia showed that the Soviets did not consider borders,
at least outside Europe, to be immutable, in contravention of
the spirit of the Helsinki Accords. The invasion led to the
US Senate's refusal to ratify the Strategic Arms Limitation
Treaty and to an American boycott of the 1980 Olympics in
Moscow, followed by the Soviet boycott of the Los Angeles
Olympics four years later. Throughout the Cold War, there
had been intermittent flare-ups around the world, interven-
tions and interference by the superpowers or their surrogates,
the repression of dissent, and expulsion of spies. Afghanistan
was different, a pure instance of territorial aggression.

Suspicions were constant, but there were no direct military confrontations between the superpowers. A *modus
vivendi* prevailed that enabled the two sides to pursue competing objectives without any real clashes. "Mutual assured

destruction" was the preferred term for avoiding the ultimate nuclear combat and the collapse of civilization.

History records the inevitability of war over territory and power struggles as regimes and ideologies rise and fall. And yet efforts persist to restrain these impulses, including the failed League of Nations and the always tenuous but enduring United Nations. The Helsinki Final Act was one such effort, though without the force of a treaty ratified by the signatories. Nonetheless, for nearly five decades it codified a norm under which the inviolability of European borders was generally observed.

What could not be known in 1975 was that the Cold War was already more than half over. It would come to a symbolic close on December 25, 1991, when the flag of the Union of Soviet Socialist Republics was lowered at the Kremlin. The Soviet Union's constituent republics and the nations of the dissolving Warsaw Pact now made their choices as independent states of how they wished to be defined—as democracies, autocracies, or some newer version of state capitalism, socialism, or even communism. In Europe, the concept of a common market evolved into a European Union, which was deemed the best means of assuring stability where there so often had not been.

The era of Helsinki lived on until February 24, 2022, when the Russian army invaded Ukraine with the proclaimed purpose of overthrowing the government there and, in effect, once again installing Russia as the ruler of this nation of forty-four million people. Vladimir Putin's declaration that he would take over another sovereign nation marked the first time in nearly seven decades that anything on that scale had happened in Europe, dwarfing Russia's incursion eight years earlier into the Donbas region and the Crimea Peninsula.

Putin had justified these prior actions by citing the regions' associations with "Mother" Russia in Slavic language, Orthodox Christianity, and family ties. In the post-Soviet period, as NATO expanded its membership to some countries bordering Russia, Putin put forward a mélange of grievances around security and his version of national histories as the reasons for the violence he unleashed. Whatever his imagined justifications, by invading Ukraine and seeking the reestablishment of Russian hegemony over its former empire, Putin was in violation of every one of the ten pledges in the Decalogue.

The Final Act itself consisted of what became known as "Baskets." The first dealt with the security issues pressed by the Soviets, including the inviolability of borders. The Kremlin wanted what amounted to a formal division of Europe based on the lands, frontiers, and water access established when World War II ended in 1945. The division of Germany into East and West, with the divided city of Berlin at its core, and sectors controlled by the Soviets, British, French, and Americans was inevitably the most sensitive issue. The prospect of the eventual reunification of Germany made these the provisions that required nuances of language that were going to be tested, one way or another, and they were.

What became clear in 2022 was that the elements making up Basket One no longer applied, at least for Putin. The European and US organizations created to monitor the accords were again invoking what had been determined in security guarantees, and the history and impact of the expansion of NATO to Eastern Europe, which could not have been anticipated in 1975.

Basket Two dealt with economic and scientific cooperation. Basket Four established a follow-up structure for monitoring compliance with the accords, a provision insisted upon by the Western democracies. Accountability was a major aspect of the West's position and the Soviets resisted the means for providing it, until they recognized it was essential.

It was Basket Three that was the most original and became, unexpectedly, the one with the most impact. (Its full text is in the appendix.) Included were all the issues on exchanges of people, information, and culture and respect for the freedoms that defined human rights, including the ability of individuals to express themselves on matters of politics, religion, and speech. The Soviets, who had initiated the call for a European Security Conference as far back as the 1950s, expected Basket Three to have minimal effect on their authoritarian rule in the Warsaw Pact nations. Instead, starting with a very small group of democratic activists in Moscow and spreading across the region and into the United States, respect for human rights as guaranteed in the Final Act became an organizing principle for dissent that would eventually become a significant factor in the implosion of Communist rule.

A historic irony is how little was expected from the Helsinki Accords from the outset of the negotiations in 1973. In particular, Henry Kissinger, Nixon and Ford's formidable national security adviser and secretary of state, was dismissive, telling Ford when he assumed office: "We never wanted it, but we went along with the Europeans . . . It is meaningless . . . It is just a grandstand play to the left." As the negotiations concluded, Ford was urged not to attend the summit. The influential *New York Times* columnist William Safire, for example, disparaged the accords before, during, and even after they were signed, advocating that they be rescinded.

The *Los Angeles Times*'s Pulitzer Prize–winning political cartoonist Paul Conrad depicted the globe on the day before, the day of, and the day after the signing as completely unchanged. This was about as positive as the reaction was in the United States.

But in Moscow a few months later, a group of dissidents, inspired by the great Soviet scientist and future Nobel Peace Prize recipient Andrei Sakharov, and led by the physicist Yuri Orlov, organized what they called the Public Group to Promote Fulfillment of the Helsinki Accords in the USSR, also known as the Moscow Helsinki Group, to monitor the Kremlin's compliance with the accords' commitments. In time, the Soviet government harassed every member of the group; exiled Sakharov and his wife, Elena Bonner, far from Moscow; jailed Orlov and Anatoly (Natan) Sharansky, another founding member; and made it impossible for the group to function.

Elsewhere in the Soviet bloc, small groups were organized and also harassed. In response, in 1978 Helsinki Watch was established in New York by four people of reputation and distinction: Robert L. Bernstein, chair of Random House; Orville Schell, a prominent lawyer; Aryeh Neier, a leading civil liberties activist; and Jeri Laber, who was to become the organization's executive director. The initial funding came from the Ford Foundation. That origin story, with permutations of personality, ingenuity, persistence, and money, is at the core of how the Final Act had lasting resonance.

Now, a half century since the origins of the Helsinki process, the concept of human rights monitoring is an established fact the world over. Helsinki Watch and its successors in the United States, the Americas, Asia, Africa, the Middle East, and later groups monitoring the rights of women, children, and others were combined in 1988 into a new umbrella organization called Human Rights Watch (HRW). Based in New York, with offices and representatives worldwide, HRW is the most important human rights nongovernmental organization in history. Its investigations, reports, and advocacy are a recognized and greatly admired gauge of the full range of political, economic, and social issues encompassed by our twenty-first century understanding of human rights.

The Helsinki Accords have retained their power even in our changing times. When they were signed in 1975, the world was well into the nuclear age, but the development of universal digital networks was in its infancy. The twentieth century was shaped by the telephone, the automobile, the airplane, radio and television, forays into space, and world wars. In summary, these were analog: tangible means and messaging as opposed to digital, which is almost entirely on screens.

Technical progress—the sweeping digital revolution of the twenty-first century, the internet, crypto culture, and the like—were imagined a half century ago but played little part in international relations. Information was distributed in the time-honored platforms of print and broadcast. The 2022 war in Ukraine shows the impact that digital images and reports can have on conflicts, by providing to the broad public an instant-by-instant understanding of what is happening. That is why the Russian government is waging a war on internal dissent and media as intense as it has waged in Ukraine itself.

Modern war is fought on the ground, in the air, and on screens, in which perceptions challenge reality for impact. The Helsinki Accords were reached in another century, but their provisions on information distribution and global standards for human rights have become ever more important because they are so much more entrenched and visible in our ways of life.

As for military conflicts, in the 1970s there were guerrilla insurgencies, anti-colonialist forces, and territorial disputes, mainly in post-colonial Africa and the Middle East. But the concept of today's cross-border, nongovernmental terrorist organizations, especially Muslim extremists, was yet to fully emerge as shaping the balance of power among nations. By contrast, in Ukraine, Vladimir Putin has unleashed a war much like those of the past: an act of aggression against a weaker neighbor. And yet its progress is measured against Helsinki's principles of human rights: how Basket Three's provisions should enable people everywhere to live a life they choose and not one that is imposed on them.

THE SUBJECT OF this book is the trajectory of the Final Act, especially the development of human rights monitoring so thorough that advocacy for changes in policy and practice were taken more seriously by governments, the media, and civil society than ever before.

The security provisions in Basket One have been the focus of multiple books by scholars and historians; they have featured NATO's enlargement and the growing recognition of Russia's—especially Vladimir Putin's—insistence that it is now surrounded by adversaries and that Europe return to the geography that prevailed after World War II. Basket One had sought to settle boundaries to the Kremlin's satisfaction.

If stories can be defined as "dog bites man" (routine) or "man bites dog" (unexpected), Basket Three of the Helsinki Accords is the latter.

What happened has unusual standing in the annals of diplomatic unexpected consequences. This saga is of courage, determination, and the ability of a small number of civilians to bring about genuine progress, against the odds.

The book is divided into chapters written by Peter Osnos and by Holly Cartner. As a correspondent in Moscow, Osnos wrote for the *Washington Post* about the Helsinki process and its consequences; he became a long-term board member of Human Rights Watch. His wife, Susan Sherer Osnos, was the first press director of Helsinki Watch in New York, and her father, Ambassador Albert W. Sherer Jr., led the American delegation to the negotiations. Cartner, a human rights lawyer who was director of the Europe and Central Asia Division of Human Rights Watch, adds her perspective on the early activities of Helsinki Watch through the years when it developed a strategy and constituency. A second chapter, a memoir, describes how Cartner, who grew up in a small North Carolina town, became a human rights professional, an investigator, and an advocate in a field that was still being devised.

The final chapters are a portrait of what Human Rights Watch has become after more than forty years. The Organization for Security and Cooperation in Europe (OSCE), based in Vienna, has been an arbiter in the Ukraine war and its aftermath along with the United Nations, the European Union, and NATO, reflecting its endurance as an institution. The US Helsinki Commission, based at the US Capitol, began as a unique collaboration between Congress and the executive branch and still plays a small role, largely outside today's partisan divides.

The Helsinki Accords have not determined the outcome of events a half century after they were signed, but their influence has been significant in establishing internationally accepted norms for state action.

The pursuit of higher human rights standards can never be completed, because it involves all the strengths of human nature that make change possible and all the weaknesses that prevent change from happening.

WOULD YOU BELIEVE ...

THE HELSINKI ACCORDS CHANGED THE WORLD?

ONE

Origins

I N THE YEARS following the end of World War II, the globe was transformed. The United States and the Soviet Union were now nuclear-armed superpowers in mortal competition. Germany was split and Japan was in ruins. Colonial powers like Britain, France, and Belgium were gradually giving way to emerging nation-states, and in an array of developing countries social, political, and economic structures were in transition. The globalization of commerce and communications was still in an analog period. The notion of a breakup of the Soviet empire seemed inconceivable. No one imagined the ascendency of China, then riven by warring factions.

Two of the strands of that post-war structure would lead in time to the Conference on Security and Cooperation in Europe. The first was that the war had ended with victors and vanquished. There was no overarching peace treaty. 'The establishment of the United Nations by charter on June 26, 1945, was a renewed effort to provide a world order that the League of Nations had been unable to sustain. Visionaries on the European continent saw the possibility of uniting the Western democracies in a way that would strengthen them collectively as an economic force and as a counterpoint to Soviet ambitions of domination. The establishment of NATO, and of the rival Warsaw Pact, made arms control and the management of military strength a necessity.

European history of the previous centuries had been marked by recurring battles over territory, with borders shifting and populations shuffled from one identity to another. The Union of Soviet Socialist Republics itself was composed of distinct nationalities from the Baltics, the Caucasus, and Central Asia and had surrounded itself with Eastern European satellites. The colossus was vast, and the Kremlin wanted its control acknowledged with, among other things, settled territorial boundaries. As the division of Europe became firm in the mid-1950s, it was the Soviets who called for a conference to enshrine in words the reality they sought on the ground.

The second strand was the realization that the global war and its aftermath had been marked by genocides, rampant persecution, discrimination against races and religions, and suppression of popular will on a scale never seen before. These were issues of historic precedence that together could be considered grievous and repeated violations of the inherent rights of all human beings.

The concept of "rights"—political, civil, economic, and social—was not new. But the notion of international standards was codified in an official way in 1948, with the United Nations General Assembly Resolution 217, the Universal Declaration of Human Rights (UDHR). The document, composed of thirty articles outlining "basic rights and fundamental freedoms," proclaims that all people are "born free and equal in dignity and rights" whatever their "nationality, place of residence, gender, national or ethnic origin, color, religion, language or any other status." The United Nations Charter forecast a document like the UDHR, and yet when it was adopted, the vote was forty-eight countries in favor, none against, and eight abstentions. Significantly, six of the abstentions were in the Soviet sphere, which resisted what came to be called "interference in the internal affairs" of nation-states.

Inevitably the goals of the declaration were tested; without force of treaty, they remained merely objectives.

In the United States, beginning most visibly with *Brown v. Board of Education*, the 1954 Supreme Court decision ending segregation in public education, a movement for civil rights of Black Americans gathered strength. These were the millions of descendants of those Africans brought to this country to be slaves, for whom racism, discrimination, inequality, bigotry, and segregation were still very much the pattern nearly a century after the Emancipation Proclamation, most notably in the southern states that had comprised the Confederacy during the Civil War.

The history of the civil rights movement has been fully explored by historians, journalists, and activists. For all the progress that would be made through legislation and practice in the 1960s and 1970s, a fundamental challenge remained: to assure equal opportunity and rights to all people whatever their identity, as enumerated in the UDHR. What became distinctive about the civil rights movement was the power of its visibility. Coinciding with the extraordinarily fast spread of television, the images of protest and suppression were now available to everyone. At their peak, the nightly network newscasts and other programming reached Americans in ways never before matched for graphic reality.

While other reasons doubtless played a role, the emphasis on civil rights evolved in the middle decades of the twentieth century into other movements, against war and nuclear arms, and for women's rights and minority rights of all kinds. American history was replete with examples of inequality and suppression of progressive activism. Never before, however, did the impact of dissent, and the government's responses to it, have so prominent a place in the awareness of the population.

Another feature of this evolution was the emergence of groups that, on the whole, were not attached to political parties and were focused on specific issues: the Student Nonviolent Coordinating Committee, the Congress of Racial Equality, and other organizations against racism; the National Organization for Women on women's issues; Amnesty International, founded in 1961, initially in support of political prisoners. Advocacy beyond ideology could be collectively understood as defending, protecting, and enabling human rights. Nongovernmental organizations (NGOs) with political and social objectives joined traditional fellowships in religion and other shared communities of spirit.

In the Soviet bloc there were regular upheavals that were put down, brutally by force, most dramatically in Hungary in 1956 and Czechoslovakia in 1968, without any intervention by the Western powers or real consequences for the Kremlin. From the Bolshevik revolution of 1917 until the collapse of the Soviet empire, the vast region the USSR held was largely kept under control by a system that successfully deployed tyranny and ersatz measures of economic development.

Civil society was not permitted in any form not dominated by the Soviet regime. And then, in 1968, Andrei Sakharov wrote an essay called "Reflections on Progress, Peaceful Coexistence and Intellectual Freedom." Coming from one of the most eminent scientists of his era, a pivotal figure in Soviet nuclear research, Sakharov's statement and his activity thereafter had a profound effect—arguably a foundation of what became the campaign for democratic ideals and reform all over the world, comparable in many ways to what was happening in the United States and Europe.

And in the aftermath of Israel's resounding victory in the 1967 Six-Day War, an increasing number of Jews in the USSR began to seek emigration to Israel. The place of Jews in Russian history was vexed. There were Jews who had played prominent roles in the Soviet ascendency, but there also existed a deep-rooted Russian tradition of virulent anti-Semitism.

For the Soviets, the Jewish emigration issue provided what became a cynical device. Jews who succeeded in getting visas could be denounced as traitors, required to pay back the cost of their education, for example. Others were denied exit on grounds that they knew one kind of state secret or another. Around the world, but especially in the United States, Jews organized on behalf of the emigration movement, which also found backing from political figures like Senator Henry Jackson, a Democrat from Washington, who combined a determination to restrain Soviet military power with a human rights doctrine of the freedom to choose where to live.

It was in this context that a long-standing Soviet call for an all-European negotiation to settle post-war boundaries began to be heard. The nations of the continent, along with the United States and Canada, were essentially formed into three groups: NATO, the Warsaw Pact, and the neutrals, which included socialist countries like Yugoslavia and small nations like Malta, the Mediterranean island state that would emerge as a disrupter of the final accords.

In the United States, the Nixon administration had been focused on bilateral relations with the Soviet Union and with the initial opening to China, while simultaneously engaged militarily in Indochina. These major issues overshadowed the early preparations for the conference, which were of little interest to the public. Joining with NATO and in quest of what were called the Mutual Balanced Force Reduction talks (a reduction of forces arrayed in Europe), the United States went along with the plans as a diplomatic ploy rather than as a full-fledged effort at an overarching peace treaty.

President Richard Nixon's national security adviser (and later secretary of state) Henry Kissinger viewed the European conference as essentially a concession to the Soviets in return for which progress on arms issues and "détente" (primarily the lessening of security tensions) might result. When Nixon held a summit with the Soviet leader Leonid Brezhnev in the late spring of 1972, a final communiqué made no mention of, in broad terms, human rights. Biographies of Kissinger and analyses of his realpolitik strategies make little or no mention of the negotiations for the accord. Nonetheless, the momentum of détente was sufficient to set the framework of what was to be called the Conference on Security and Cooperation in Europe (CSCE).

Foreign ministers from thirty-five nations met in Helsinki in July 1973 to begin work on a general agreement, and they agreed to reconvene in Geneva that September. Albania, at the time an outlier in Europe and aligned with China, was the only European country that refused to participate.

As an international forum of this size, and considering that the eventual impact was far greater than the original expectations, CSCE had a dynamic well worth exploring and understanding.

TWO

To Helsinki

D
IPLOMATIC HISTORY BY its nature tends not to be enthralling, especially when the topic is the intricacy of more than two years of meetings among thirty-five nations to reach agreement on language for an accord to be signed by the leaders of all these countries at an international conference. Each word had the possibility of being disputed, and a great many were.

To appreciate the scope of the Final Act, the full text runs more than seventy pages in agate type, and in the course of negotiating the precise language, each country approached

---

The definitive book on the Conference of Security and Cooperation in Europe is *To Helsinki: The Conference on Security and Cooperation in Europe, 1973–1975* by Ambassador John J. Maresca, who held major positions at NATO and in the US delegation to CSCE. Published by Duke University Press in 1985 and updated in later versions, it is indispensable to the history of the accords as recorded by an American participant with scholarly and writing skills. Much of this chapter is drawn from that book, with permission of the publisher.

the ten principles of the Decalogue from the perspective of its own national self-interest and ideology. Two issues were especially complex: the "inviolability" of national borders and the grounds for "interference" into a country's internal affairs, the euphemism for monitoring compliance with human rights standards.

On both these matters, and despite the American insistence that it was adopting a low-key approach to its role in the conference (out of deference to the Europeans and the belief in Washington, DC, that the CSCE process was of more benefit to the Soviets than to the United States), in the end the US engagement was critical to the outcome.

It was Henry Kissinger who managed to unravel these tangles despite his basic condescension about the process, in part because of his working relations with Soviet foreign minister Andrei Gromyko, with whom he had met one-on-one as part of the détente process. On the frontiers issue, central to the Soviet interest in CSCE, the core question was how to leave open the possibility of the reunification of Germany.

East and West Germany had already developed as two nations with a common history and language and two distinct political alliances. The operating language appeared to make that division permanent: "The participating States regard as inviolable one another's frontiers as well as the frontiers of all States in Europe and therefore will refrain now and in the future from assaulting these frontiers. Accordingly, they will also refrain from any demand for, or act of seizure and usurpation of part or all of the territory of any participating state."

The breakthrough came in a session between Kissinger and Gromyko in Geneva in February 1975, where the necessary adjustments in language were made. For a pan-European conference, the future of Germany was by historical measures an essential topic. And yet the future of a country responsible for two world wars in the twentieth century was in the wording agreed by the two superpowers, not by the country itself. After intense deliberation that Kissinger called "abstruse and esoteric," this sentence was added: "The participating States consider that their frontiers can be changed only in accordance with international law through peaceful means and by agreement."

The territorial doctrine was not effectively breached in Europe until 2014, when Russia annexed Crimea with military force and resisted any pressure to relent. That war then expanded to a full invasion in 2022, when Russia recognized the independence of the Donbas and launched a ground, air, and sea offensive against its neighbor. In 1975, it was beyond any imagining that the breakup of the USSR would add so many nation-states to Europe and Central Asia, each with its own ethnic, regional, and social order. In revisiting the way Soviet republics were viewed by the rest of the world when they were part of the USSR, the Soviet Union was invariably called "Russia" and its people (of whatever ethnicity) were "Russians." Ignored were the facts that the Soviet dictator Joseph Stalin was Georgian and that Leonid Brezhnev's birthplace, Kamenskoye, was in Ukraine. Examples of these national identity misnomers were multiple.

The concept of a Union of Soviet Socialist Republics with fifteen constituent states, each ostensibly with the right to secede, and smaller autonomous republics primarily composed of ethnic groups was largely deemed irrelevant. All of these were subservient to Russia, including the Baltic states of Latvia, Lithuania, and Estonia, whose absorption into the USSR in 1940 had never been recognized by the West. At the founding of the United Nations in 1945, Moscow demanded fifteen seats in the General Assembly and settled for three: one for the USSR as a whole and one each for Ukraine and Byelorussia. It was as though the United States had asked for fifty seats before agreeing to the one.

Conflict also emerged over Basket Three, the range of topics labeled "humanitarian and cultural cooperation." In contemporary jargon these are the "soft power" ways in which people benefit from the free exchanges of culture, information, and movement. Underlying these is a much more profound matter, the way governments and regimes relate to their populations on all manner of rights.

The autocratic view was that each country's hold over its citizenry was beyond challenge by any other. The democratic position was that civil and political rights were valid matters for international monitoring. The Helsinki Accords would need to straddle those positions to reach the required consensus conclusion. As Ambassador John Maresca writes: "There is no doubt that the Basket Three experiment . . . was the most original element of the CSCE negotiations."

For the United States and the Soviet Union, the issues of Basket Three were not a major focus as the conference began. A first principle of the formal document agreed by the two countries in 1972 said this: "Differences in ideology and in social systems of the USA and the USSR are not obstacles to the bilateral development of normal relations based on the principles of sovereignty, equality, noninterference in internal affairs and mutual advantage."

At the same Geneva session between Kissinger and Gromyko that devised the language about national borders, Kissinger raised the more contentious Basket Three issues. "The questions were so complicated," Maresca observes, "the number and variety of countries and national interests so broad and the various interrelated negotiating problems so tangled that only the negotiators themselves, on the spot in Geneva, could see through to possible solutions."

What Kissinger apparently believed was that the Soviet Union, whose position would also determine that of other Warsaw Pact countries, recognized that unless human rights provisions were in the final document, the Western nations would never agree to the territorial provisions. As Maresca writes: "On questions such as human rights, which touched on the very basis of our civilization, the Western negotiators were in fundamental agreement. The group of middle grade diplomats understood instinctively and unanimously the concepts they could not, under any circumstances, compromise. Sometimes their judgment necessarily turned on the nuance of an adjective or the sequence of a series of phrases; in each case the limit was clear."

Having publicly demonstrated at the superpower level—in the 1972 Moscow summit declaration, for example—that human rights were not a core issue for bilateral relations between the United States and the Soviet Union, Kissinger could imply that references to these matters were a modest concession to the lesser players at the conference. "The Soviets concluded," writes Maresca, "that the results of negotiations [on Basket Three] would be quickly forgotten and that US political figures had no interest in maintaining human rights pressures." Neither Washington nor Moscow could have predicted that the coming presidency of Jimmy Carter and the astounding courage of a small group of Soviet and Eastern European dissidents would make human rights language the most important of the resolutions in the comprehensive and very densely worded agreement.

IN THE EARLY 1970s, a spiral of events was underway in the
United States that would define the nation's character in
ways unprecedented in its history.

The Indochina wars were gradually unwinding, at least for
American forces, and a defeat for the US side in the conflicts
was predictable, although not yet a fact. What had been battles to forestall communism in Southeast Asia were actually
civil wars that outside powers had neither the ability nor the
will to resolve.

The action-reaction cycles to the American anti-war
movement—the deaths at Kent State of four protesters, for
instance—and the Nixon administration's peace process with
a subtext of a "decent interval" before giving up to the North
Vietnamese injected a measure of popular cynicism about
governments that has never subsided.

Watergate, a spectacular collision of political chicanery
and cover-up exposed by an increasingly powerful national
media, was much more exciting than a negotiation over words
for an agreement that almost no one in the United States even
knew was underway and even fewer cared much about. Those
doing the bargaining were there because that was their job,
not on some providential mission.

Wars, elections, revolutions, pandemics, economic ups
and downs all have consequences that can be measured. Treaties among nations require ratification by legislatures or some
other form of official recognition. With so much else of importance happening, the CSCE negotiations were virtually
invisible. Concerted research into news coverage of the deliberations returns very few stories in databases. In the *Washington Post* of June 22, 1974, I found one piece of my own. More
than a year before the signing summit, I wrote: "Even what
has been agreed upon—and a number of important points are

already in draft form—must still be finalized. Since everything must be done by consensus, any one country (San Marino if it wanted to) could slow things down further."

As it happens, it was Dom Mintoff of Malta, the small island nation, who brought the conference to a stalemate in its final weeks a year later. At issue were the security interests of the Mediterranean countries. Maresca gives a sense of the convoluted deliberations as time was running out: "By the time the Coordinating Committee had convened at noon, it had become apparent that the Maltese would not accept the Canadian proposal. The Maltese were also blocking agreement on the follow-up document. The Romanians in turn would not lift their reservation on the quadripartite rights clause until the follow-up document was complete and the FRG [West Germany] would not agree, even conditionally, to a Stage Three date until the quadripartite rights clause had been agreed."

I was told that diplomats from other countries began referring to the Maltese politician as "Dumb" Mintoff.

The official American stance toward these deliberations, as I wrote in my article, was "low key" or low profile, except when Kissinger and Gromyko settled issues to get to those they really cared about. What did that mean?

When the first phase of CSCE was agreed in 1973, the US delegation was led by George Vest, a career Foreign Service Officer with enough self-confidence to manage his role as a lesser presence than was typical for an American. He did not ask for an ambassadorial title, although other delegation leaders had them. Maresca writes that Vest was "extremely clever at using a combination of personal prestige and Yankee common sense to exercise a major influence on events." Maresca adds that, with a rural Virginia background, Vest compared the conference to "leading a team of mules. It was always hard to get them pulling together."

After Vest left to become the State Department spokesman and another diplomat served briefly in the top post, Albert W. Sherer Jr. was named to lead the delegation through the two years when the document moved from concept to reality. Ambassador Sherer had a classic résumé for a Foreign Service Officer of his generation.

He had attended Yale and Harvard Law School, served as a navigator in the US Army Air Corps in the Pacific during World War II, shared an office with future president Gerald R. Ford preparing for the bar exam, and then joined the Foreign Service, where he served until his retirement about thirty years later. His last professional role was as a lawyer in a legal assistance clinic connected with Northwestern University Law School.

He died in Christmas week of 1986 of cancer. His widow, Carroll Russell Sherer, who had been an invaluable partner to her husband in Morocco, Hungary, Czechoslovakia, Poland, Togo, Guinea, and Washington, lived on successfully as an interior designer; she died at age eighty-nine in 2012 in Greenwich, Connecticut.

I know all this because my wife, Susan, was the middle of the Sherers' three children. A half century later, it is still remarkable to me that as a journalist I was a reporter about the Helsinki process, and my father-in-law was responsible for the US role. In addition, Susan's uncle Harold Russell was a State Department lawyer assigned to be the legal adviser to the US delegation in the critical drafting stages.

Ambassador Sherer and I were at two ends of the spectrum on Helsinki-related matters: handling the negotiations and judging them from a distance. The potential for a conflict of interests was never discussed by us, which I attribute to a combination of the ambassador's professionalism and the fact that CSCE did not merit coverage in the American media as a source of controversy. One measure of what it meant to be simultaneously the US ambassador in Prague and the head of delegation in Geneva, where the bargaining was happening, was the respective residences in the two cities.

In Prague, the residence was a palace, one of the most impressive of any such domiciles in the diplomatic world. It had been the home of a very wealthy Jewish family who had fled the country at the start of World War II, and decades later it was still as grand as it had been then. In Geneva, Ambassador and Mrs. Sherer shared an apartment so small (although elegant) that they slept on a Murphy bed lowered from the wall every evening.

As Maresca details and as Harold Russell has confirmed in conversations recently, the policy advisories from Washington were few and usually vague enough to leave tactics and strategy up to the team on the ground. The essential guidance was "do no harm." By joining on every meaningful topic with the NATO countries, the possibilities of any disputes among them would be minor. And as far as the Soviets were concerned, the objective was to manage their aspirations to make them satisfactory to the Kremlin but simultaneously acceptable to its adversaries.

Maresca's portrait of Ambassador Sherer was, in my view as his son-in-law, a good one. The ambassador arrived at CSCE as the negotiations were gathering momentum: "He had no direct knowledge of the CSCE [but] he had prestige as the serving US ambassador to Prague and long experience dealing with the communist world. The low profile suited his personal style, but he gradually developed a position of useful influence within the conference by projecting the image of a 'wise man' who was somewhat above the petty maneuvering of the negotiations."

As a career diplomat rather than the representative of a country in the Eastern bloc with goals set by the Kremlin, Sherer could navigate among the interests of the Western democracies, without strict adherence to Washington instructions, in large part because there were so few of them. In later stages of the CSCE process (a follow-up conference in Belgrade and another conference years later in Madrid), the US delegations were led by major political figures, the former Supreme Court justice Arthur Goldberg and Max Kampelman, whose mandate was to demand Soviet adherence to human rights commitments. Their appointments were proof that the CSCE had moved from the diplomatic sphere to the political one, a part of the Cold War contest of ideals.

Had either of these men or their counterparts from other countries been in the negotiations for the accords, it is very likely they would never have been reached. The lighter touch of Sherer, Maresca, and the "experts" on the American team enabled the Soviets to accept provisions in Basket Three whose potential impact they clearly did not appreciate.

After Nixon's resignation and Gerald Ford's accession to the presidency, the tenor of détente began to change. In November 1974, Ford met Brezhnev in Vladivostok for a summit in which progress on strategic arms control was made. This was the only topic to be discussed and it seemed to me, as an American reporter based in Moscow, that progress would be a major step in the stability of superpower relations. But soon thereafter Brezhnev disappeared from view, and it was subsequently learned that his health had begun a long physical (and eventually mental) decline. For the *Washington Post*, I wrote a story in January that began this way:

> Last Friday night, the Moscow correspondent of the Press Trust of India reported that Soviet Communist Party leader Leonid Brezhnev had "taken leave of his responsibilities" and was recovering in a dacha outside Moscow from effects of a nagging respiratory problem. In New Delhi, the correspondent of Agence France-Presse misunderstood the Indian dispatch and quoting the Moscow story reported that Brezhnev had resigned.
>
> By Saturday morning, half the Western correspondents in the Soviet capital, alerted by their home offices about the AFP bulletin, were chasing the resignation rumor. It was that kind of month in Moscow.

Brezhnev, of course, had not resigned. But in my sense of things, that flap marked a change in the mood of détente, if not yet the substance.

In the course of 1975, as the negotiations in Geneva moved forward in minuscule increments, other developments were shadowing the Soviet-American relationship. When the United States granted the Soviets most-favored-nation trading status, Congress enacted what was known as the Jackson-Vanik Amendment, which made this status contingent on the level of Jewish emigration as a human rights issue. From my perspective in Moscow and later in retrospect, I felt that emigration was used by all sides for purposes beyond the right to choose where to live.

As noted, emigration from the USSR was at the center of the human rights movement there. The rights involved were indisputable: people choosing where to live, when their

current situation was inhospitable. And yet cynicism was
the subtext of debate. The Soviets adjusted the numbers of
visas to suit their short-term interests. Long-standing anti-
Semitism meant that the Kremlin could use Jewish emigration to confirm popular attitudes toward Jewish nationalism.
Senator Jackson and his allies in Congress saw the amendment as a way to weaken détente because of their belief that
the Soviets were a continuing profound security and ideological threat.

And finally, as time went on, the numbers of Jews ostensibly leaving for Israel for religious reasons shifted to many
choosing to go to the United States instead, largely as a way
to enhance their personal freedoms and lifestyles. Eventually,
about one million Soviet Jews made it to Israel. But a very
large number went to the United States, settling in places like
Brighton Beach in Brooklyn and establishing a community
with distinctly Russian business, cultural, and culinary styles.

Throughout history, emigration and immigration have
had many causes and consequences. In the era of the Helsinki
Accords, these were often tactical, meaning expedient as well
as humanitarian. Israel wanted and needed the Soviet immigrants. Yet the growing tension over Israel's frustration with
the trend toward so many immigrants heading elsewhere did
not surface in any meaningful way. To make immigration a
political issue might have shifted the balance of support in the
United States, which had cast the exodus as a religious choice
rather than, as it often was, a lifestyle one.

In the CSCE negotiations, political considerations under-
scored what in rhetorical exchanges were said to be purely about
principle. Ultimately, the Soviet bloc wanted to be strengthened by provisions in the Final Act, whereas the Western
countries had a different goal: to weaken the authoritarian

hold over people in the communist East by whatever means possible.

The disgrace of Richard Nixon and the sordid departure of his vice president, Spiro Agnew, meant that the United States in 1975 was led by an unelected president, Gerald Ford, and an appointed vice president, Nelson Rockefeller. The standing of the United States as a paragon of democracy was, not surprisingly, diminished. And in the spring of that year, Cambodia and Vietnam fell to the "enemies" of US policy. While the continued presence of Kissinger suggested continuity at the administration's pinnacle, the détente strategy became harder to justify to a world public that saw little moral difference between the two superpowers. After all, the United States had gone to Indochina to stop the spread of communism, but in 1972 Nixon had exchanged toasts with Mao Zedong in Beijing.

The shift in attitudes was increasingly on display. In April 1975, speaking to the American Society of Newspaper Editors, Kissinger declared, "We must continue our policy of seeking to ease tensions. But we shall insist that the easing of tensions cannot occur selectively. We shall never forget who supplied the arms which North Vietnam used to make a mockery of its signature on the Paris Accords," which by then, as Kissinger acknowledged, were no longer "relevant."

In that same speech, Kissinger said: "We must give up on the illusion that foreign policy can choose between morality and pragmatism. America cannot be true to itself unless it upholds humane values and the dignity of the individual . . . The American people must never forget that our strength gives force to our principles and our principles give purpose to our strength."

This revised approach was dramatically displayed when President Ford chose not to meet with the recently exiled

Soviet writer and Nobel laureate Alexandr Solzhenitsyn at the White House in June, which Kissinger eventually acknowledged was because of its "symbolic effect," and not, as had been asserted, because of scheduling problems. Meanwhile, the writer had been fêted everywhere else in Washington, and the White House was seen as being submissive to the Kremlin.

In continental Europe, particularly in France, Italy, and Portugal, communist parties were making inroads in some elections, which was, not surprisingly, alarming. In hindsight, the notion of a Marxist sweep in southern Europe was exaggerated and the parties were essentially socialists with awe-inspiring names. Their adherents ranged from Marxist-Leninists like Dolores Ibárruri of Spain, known as *La Pasionaria*, who returned from exile in Moscow in 1977, to Italy's Enrico Berlinguer, whose Italian Communist Party nonetheless broke with the USSR.

Meanwhile, the laborious negotiating process was continuing in Geneva with the expectation that a summit of the thirty-five signatories could be scheduled for Helsinki at the end of July. But for that to happen, a frenetic round of give-and-take over language, especially on Basket Three, was necessary.

With their long-standing goal of setting territorial boundaries finally in view, the Soviet delegation accepted that human rights issues had to be a core element of the Final Act. By its end, Maresca concludes, the "interrelated series of clauses and provisions [came] closer to the objectives of the West than . . . the interests of the Soviet Union."

As the last details of the accords were finally resolved, and all thirty-five heads of state agreed to gather in Helsinki for the ceremonial signing, the interest in the United States about

the accords, such as it was, was critical. "Far from congrat-
ulating often courageous negotiators for a Western achievement," Maresca writes, "the Western press almost universally
vilified the Final Act." The title of an editorial in the *Wall
Street Journal* was "Jerry Don't Go."

As was often the case in the Cold War years, events were
invariably presented in the media and by politicians as part of
an endless zero-sum power competition. The interpretation
of the accords as "a favor to Brezhnev" was similar in theme
to the arguments long made that Soviet nuclear power and
weaponry were greater than those of the United States. The
détente years had a somewhat moderated tone, but in 1975 the
most vituperative American arguments again saw any compromise as inexorable weakness.

And in truth, President Ford, whose understanding of the
East-West dynamic was not sophisticated, never did grasp the
meaning of CSCE. Running for election against Jimmy Carter in 1976, Ford badly fumbled a debate question, leaving the
impression—impossible for him to clarify—that he did not
understand or could not explain the control the Kremlin had
over its Eastern European satellites. Poland, he said, was not
actually dominated by the Soviets, an assertion condemned
as ignorance. What I thought he meant to say was that the
strength of the Catholic Church, among other national traits,
gave Poles a semblance of defiance.

The subtleties of human rights language were similarly
impenetrable to most American politicians and pundits. So
Ford traveled to Helsinki under a cloud, a popular reaction
that ranged from a lack of interest to outright opposition.

In the days before the scheduled summit on July 31 and
August 1, a space mission was underway called Apollo-Soyuz,
in which astronauts from the United States and the Soviet

Union were to link up their vehicles in space, a symbol of peaceful collaboration. That mission went off as planned, and in some of the positive coverage of equals in space was the subtext that Soviet technology was actually primitive compared to its American counterpart.

Looking at news coverage of the summit and reading the speeches of Ford and Brezhnev, the spectacle is there, as well as how superficial the substance seemed to be, an interlude in high summer with a lot of limousines and pomp. The headline of *Time* magazine's cover story was "Showtime in Helsinki . . . Gerald Ford, Leonid Brezhnev, and an All-Star Cast in 'Goodbye to World War II.'" The image was altered to show Ford and Brezhnev in what appeared to be a dance floor two-step, reinforcing the sense that the United States was dancing to the Soviets' tune. "Others thought of it as Dreams of Détente," the magazine continued. "Still others would call it Much Ado about Nothing or perhaps even The Decline of the West." *Time*'s chief European correspondent, William Rademakers, offered this assessment:

> The vast majority of Eastern Europeans appear to be either indifferent or cynical about the Security Conference. At worst, they regard it as an extension of the 1945 Yalta Conference which delivered Eastern Europe into the Soviet sphere. At best, they acknowledge that it puts some pressure on Communist regimes to answer travel restrictions, gives easier access to Western information, and perhaps slightly widens the room for maneuver between the Soviet and East European brands of communism. There are no longer any illusions in Eastern Europe about crusades for freedom . . . in the absence of

any hope for political freedom, they have turned to the pursuit of materialistic goals; a summer cottage, a Japanese stereo set or—the greatest of all communist status goals—a new car.

The conclusion of the piece, quoting a State Department official, is this: "There's no court to take anybody into, but this document gives us some moral authority for saying, 'You agreed. Why are you not living up to your word?'" and then, "The big show in Helsinki is unlikely to cause much harm and may well do more than a little good."

One of the last contentious issues to be resolved before the summit was how to manage "accountability." Once again, the East and West blocs had differing views on what that should mean. The eventual consensus was expressed by Yugoslavia's leader Josip Broz Tito, who said: "The present conference does not mark the end but the beginning of a process . . . We must not fail to take advantage of the opportunities we have created with considerable effort. That is our great responsibility which we have to face jointly."

Initially the Soviets favored a follow-up plan but backed away when it became evident that adherence to provisions in the Final Act could be measured. According to Maresca, NATO also had to be persuaded that further review would give CSCE more validity. Finally, a meeting was agreed to be held in Belgrade in 1977 with, he writes, "a mandate to exchange views on both the implementation and on the possible deepening of their mutual relations . . . and the process of détente in the future."

At the close of the summit, as the leaders rushed off to catch their flights home, Maresca recalls:

Many of the diplomats who had negotiated the document gathered for a farewell dinner in an eighteenth-century manor house deep in the Finnish forest. They had spent two years together in difficult, sometimes bitter, discussions. The night was warm and the mood of the group philosophical.

"Well, they signed it," said one.

"And now it will be buried and forgotten," said another.

"No," replied a third, "You are wrong. We have started something."

History would show that this was the correct appraisal.

THREE

Dissidents Take the Helsinki Accords at Their Word

THE YEARS FROM 1975 to 1991 were an instant in historical time, but that is all it took for the world that existed at Helsinki to be restructured in ways that were, if not inconceivable when the Final Act was signed, largely unimaginable, as if the mighty Roman Empire had imploded in less than two decades. And, strikingly, the upheaval came about without violence of any significant kind.

In 1975, the total population of the Soviet Union was about 250 million people. America's population was about 215 million. But the USSR's gross domestic product was about half that of the United States. As nuclear powers, their military capacities were constantly being measured with the American tendency—a political asset in most elections—to imply that the Soviets were at least equal if not superior in strategic or tactical forces.

Many terms are used to describe the end of the Soviet empire: implosion, collapse, dissolution. In a way, they are all correct. Historians and political scientists compile the records in economics, the fundamental inefficiency of state-controlled industry and agriculture; corruption, the inability of states to reform their leadership and bureaucracies; and socially meaningful developments, such as the ascension of Pope John Paul II, which galvanized the overwhelmingly Roman Catholic population of Poland, the largest of the Kremlin satellites; or perhaps most important of all, the fall of the Berlin Wall in 1989, which led to the reunification of Germany, recreating the nation in Europe's center that had determined the dynamic in Europe so dramatically in the twentieth century.

According to Andrei Grachev, an astute adviser to Gorbachev as the USSR unraveled, the perceptions of why the Soviet Union disappeared among "Western political leaders and analysts" are too narrow. In his book *Gorbachev's Gamble: Soviet Foreign Policy and the End of the Cold War*, he writes that the standard explanation is "more or less summarized in the formula of Michael R. Beschloss and Strobe Talbott in their book *At the Highest Levels*. They argue that the improvements in the Kremlin's behavior were a direct result of forty years of consistent pressure from the West and particularly for the previous eight years from the Reagan administration. . . .

"This amounts to a rather simplistic reading of an extremely complicated and controversial historical episode," Grachev writes, presenting an alternative explanation that he considers to be equal to the pressures of the arms race: "It was the 'managed cohabitation' which in different forms—from [German chancellor] Willy Brandt's *Ostpolitik* to the provisions of the Helsinki Final Act—managed to stage a trap for the Soviet leaders, obliging them to compete with the West not just in the field of weapons production, where their system proved to be quite efficient, but also in a totally different area.

The Soviet Union proved unable to compete when it came to assuring individual freedom and civil rights or, above all, the creation of decent conditions for everyday life.

"It was largely this policy that eventually led to the internal decomposition of the Soviet monolith, giving birth to the viruses of pro-Western reformist currents," Grachev states. Without specifically endorsing this explanation, he writes: "The shell was bound to crack."

For the purposes of this narrative, the focus is on the way that Basket Three in the Final Act codified human rights, providing a means to measure whether states were adhering to the standards and practices they had agreed to follow. From the Bolshevik revolution in 1917 and the Soviet takeover of Eastern Europe after World War II, opposition to official order was crushed—as far back as the 1950s in East Germany and Hungary, the 1960s in Poland and Czechoslovakia, and of course in the Soviet Union itself, where after the Stalin era of mass purges, any public dissent or (in the outer reaches of the empire) signs of nationalism could be stifled with barely more than a shake or two of the KGB's formidable fist.

The center of dissent was in Russia. It was by far the largest entity in the Soviet empire, and the Russian language and Communist Party orthodoxies overwhelmed all else across the country's eleven time zones. The Baltics, the Caucasus, and the Central Asian republics all had elements of opposition that were largely outside the scope of international visibility. Most of the world accepted that Estonia, Ukraine, Georgia, and Kazakhstan were now melded into a single vast and powerful system run from the Kremlin by a small group of men and the security apparatus they directed.

The identifiable dissidents in Moscow never numbered more than a few hundred people (there was no census of them), leaving aside the hundreds of thousands of Jews who sought to emigrate. But the dissidents were visible and accessible, their activities and the repression of them were magnified in the West, and the assumption was that they were the vanguard of a much larger population of people aggrieved by Soviet autocracy and repression.

After 1975, in Moscow, Leningrad, Poland, and Czechoslovakia, dissident groups were formed; the core of their organizing principles, which proved over time to be so important, were the provisions solemnly and in detail agreed in the Helsinki Accords.

I N 1975, THE status of discontent and the group of Soviet citizens prepared to express it publicly, known collectively as "dissidents," was if anything a minor nuisance for the Kremlin. More than a half century of Soviet hegemony had successfully suppressed any opposition that would be taken seriously outside the country. The World War II alliance against Nazism, which evolved into the Cold War, was essentially considered a contest between the superpower blocs. Little consideration was given to the possibility of organic change in the USSR and the Warsaw Pact, in part because the successive efforts at demanding reform could so easily be crushed.

The widespread purges in the Stalin era of supposed enemies of the state had evolved across the empire into politically motivated arrests, intimidations, and heavy-handed bureaucratic ploys that mostly defined the years after Nikita Khrushchev's "secret speech" of 1956. Russian was the lingua franca of a nation of more than one hundred nationalities. Recognition of dissent in the West came mainly from controversies surrounding literature, as with Boris Pasternak's banned novel

Doctor Zhivago or Alexandr Solzhenitsyn's *The Gulag Archipelago*. These books reverberated far more in the West than they ever could in the USSR or the satellites.

The domestic power of the KGB and its counterparts elsewhere was more pervasive than purely sinister, as in Stalin's years, or even brutal. Every entity of any consequence was, one way or another, infiltrated or influenced by the state's priorities of control. The techniques ranged from sophisticated espionage to cruelly cynical, sending people to mental asylums where they were drugged into submission. But by and large, they were not as lethal as the mass executions of the empire's first four decades.

The USSR played at the highest levels of international policy and military power, and most of its people (historians and journalists seemed to agree) accepted their fate and expected it to be eternal. Not, however, the dissidents. We now know, of course, that the apparent quiescence and stability of the Soviet Union was misleading, based on the fact that barely more than decade later, when Mikhail Gorbachev became party secretary and devised *glasnost* and *perestroika*—meant to modernize communism, not eliminate it—the state so soon unraveled. Among imperial downfalls, the disappearance of the Soviet Union was perhaps the fastest and least bloody. Not until 2022, when Vladimir Putin invaded Ukraine and made explicit the intention of reviving Russian hegemony over what had been the realm of empire, had that possibility been really considered.

If there had been no Helsinki Final Act, the Soviet Union and the satellites might well have dissolved over time through the internal contradictions of economic inadequacy and ideological contradictions, just as in czarist times an elite ruled peasants and serfs until the Bolshevik revolution ended that epoch. The boundaries and reach of Russia and surrounding territories were ruled from a fortress. The nobility never pretended, however, to represent the people, which was, ultimately, the greatest fallacy of the communists.

IN THE FINE print of the Final Act and its accompanying agreements was a provision that mandated publication of the full document by the signatories. In Moscow, *Pravda* (the most official of Soviet newspapers) ran the full text. Elsewhere in the bloc, publication was dutifully done. It is hard to imagine that readers inundated with official propaganda and rhetoric paid much attention.

Western newspapers, subject to commercial imperatives, almost certainly never did more than summarize the accords. It is a safe bet that the actual readers of Basket Three were very few. Fortunately, those readers included a group of dissidents in Moscow.

Somewhere the myth emerged that it was publication of the accords in the Soviet papers that immediately prompted the establishment of a monitoring group. According to Natan Sharansky, one of the founders and probably the last surviving member of the group, the origins were two visits to Moscow by members of Congress, one before the summit and the second shortly after. Whatever may have been said, what the listeners heard was that the Final Act contained language worth attention. Rhetorical declarations of reform by the Kremlin tended to be ignored even by its critics, but in this instance the validation of American political figures provided some credibility.

A case can be made that if the Soviet Jews and their supporters had not coalesced around the issue of emigration, the extent of Western awareness of the human rights issues would have been far less resonant. The scale of support for Jewish emigration, particularly in the United States, was in a different category of attention, capable of drawing crowds and raising money and impressing politicians who saw the combination of appeal to their constituents and another way to assail Soviet policies across the board.

When in 1974 the Kremlin imposed a clearly punitive "education tax" on applicants for exit visas, Senator Henry Jackson and Representative Charles Vanik succeeded in making "most-favored-nation" trade benefits for the Soviets contingent on the rate of emigration. The use of this kind of "leverage" with the Soviets and "linkage" of benefits to concessions or compromise added another kind of condition to the Nixon-Kissinger pursuit of détente on the issues of security and strategic arms negotiations. With the Helsinki Accords containing language pledging "respect for human rights and fundamental freedoms," there was a basis for measuring compliance that the Soviets had underestimated and would at least have to recognize, even as they violated those rights and freedoms.

In his 2020 memoir *Never Alone: Prison, Politics, and My People*, Sharansky vividly describes a meeting with a bipartisan delegation of fourteen visiting US senators in the summer of 1975, a group led by Hubert Humphrey and Hugh Scott that also included Abe Ribicoff and Jacob Javits, both of whom were Jewish.

A meeting was arranged at the Rossiya Hotel, where the delegation was staying, and a group of "refuseniks" (as Jews denied visas were called) was convened and made it through security. Humphrey and Scott did not attend, not wanting to have their meeting with Leonid Brezhnev cancelled, but the other senators did. Among the messages delivered to the refuseniks was that an agreement containing human rights issues, including emigration provisions, was about to be concluded in Helsinki.

Sharansky writes that the importance of this meeting was confirmed during his indictment and trial in 1977, when his role as an organizer was one of the nineteen episodes classified as "high treason," with a potential death sentence.

Initially, the small group of democracy dissidents (as distinct from would-be emigrants) considered Helsinki a Western failure because the Soviets would never comply with its requirements on human rights. Sharansky, who had an unusual role among the refuseniks because he also had close relations with non-Jewish activists like Yuri Orlov, Lyudmila Alexeyeva, and Andrei Amalrik, writes that they had many heated debates, "wondering how we could hold the Soviet Union to these new commitments."

In September, a delegation of House members came to Moscow. Given the upbeat tenor of the moment they were housed at the Hotel Sovietskaya, where only honored guests were admitted. The members invited the refuseniks to the hotel, where they were closely observed by the KGB but were left undisturbed. In this session, the visitors emphasized the value of the Final Act language, which, Sharansky recalls, again made an impact on the listeners.

One glimpse at the dynamics of the past was that a woman showing particular interest in the discussion was thought to be a secretary. She turned out to be Representative Millicent Fenwick, a New Jersey Republican who would soon establish the Commission on Security and Cooperation in Europe, a bipartisan group of members of Congress with the authority to oversee how the signatories of the accord, most specifically the Soviet bloc, met its provisions. Fenwick was a colorful personality. She smoked an elegant pipe and had a bearing and manner more akin to Katharine Hepburn than a traditional politician.

Back in Moscow, the accords started to be considered in a new way. Sharansky said that he proposed to his friends appealing to politicians, media, and human rights organizations to uphold "the spirit of Helsinki." Orlov, who had made a public declaration in support of Andrei Sakharov as early as 1973, was by instinct more combative than Sharansky, whose personality enabled him to straddle the predictably fractious relationships of those brave enough to be dissenters. Orlov proposed establishing a monitoring group with the intention of tracking and publicizing Soviet infractions of the human rights provisions.

The concept of a monitoring process on human rights was not altogether new. In his 2022 book *The Quiet Before,* Gal Beckerman describes how, starting in 1968, Natalia Gorbanevskaya adapted the *samizdat* practice of sharing material that could not be published in typewritten manuscripts, in what became known as the *Chronicle of Current Events.* This was a collection of news from around the country about activists who defied the state in a variety of ways and were punished. It was widely read and noticed in the West. In issue No. 18, Beckerman writes, the following item appeared: "On 9 January 1971, Natalya Gorbanevskaya was transferred from Butyrka Prison to the Special Psychiatric Hospital on Sechenov Street in Kazan . . . where a course of treatment with Haloperidol had been prescribed for her." After her release she emigrated to France and took Polish citizenship. She died in 2013.

Around that same time, another physicist and social scientist, Valery Chalidze, had established what was called the

Moscow Human Rights Committee with Andrei Sakharov and a few other activists. Its mission was to provide information and counsel to people who believed their rights were being violated. The committee utilized the various means of reaching people throughout the country with *samizdat* distribution of its findings and engaging with Western journalists ready to publicize the reports abroad. Radio Liberty (the CIA-sponsored broadcast station) and the Russian service of the Voice of America (VOA) played back the news to listeners able to circumvent the jamming that was standard.

In 1972, Chalidze visited the United States on a lecture tour, and the Kremlin revoked his Soviet citizenship. He and several other exiled activists, with access to private American funding, started Khronika Press, which published reports and books under the banner "A Chronicle of Human Rights in the USSR." With the perspective of a half century, the capacity to collect and release such information was the opening step in organized resistance to the regime, moving beyond the realm of pressing the boundaries in literature, as Solzhenitsyn and Pasternak had done.

In the winter of 1976, Orlov and Sharansky joined with a dozen or so other dissidents in what they called the Public Group to Promote Fulfillment of the Helsinki Accords in the USSR, which became known as the Moscow Helsinki Group. Andrei Sakharov's small apartment was the venue for press conferences, although it was his wife, Elena Bonner, who was actually a founding member.

Other members of the group included Lyudmila Alexeyeva, a writer and activist who stayed on in the Soviet Union, came to the United States, and later returned; she was still going strong as a critic of the post-Soviet government when she died in Moscow in 2018 at age ninety-one.

She was venerated for her stalwart clarity of vision and for never giving up.

Petro Grigorenko was a high-ranking decorated army officer of Ukrainian descent. He spent years incarcerated in mental hospitals, although he was never mentally ill. He finally made it to the United States, where he died in 1987 at the age of seventy-nine.

Anatoly Marchenko was another writer-activist whose public dissent was especially fierce. He died in prison in 1987 after a three-month hunger strike. He was forty-eight years old.

Just listing these names underscores how extraordinary it was that such a disparate group of so very few people would join together to take on the Kremlin and believe that they might survive, let alone succeed.

This Helsinki group's intent was not specifically about Jewish emigration, although Sharansky was instrumental in launching it. As he writes in *Never Alone:* "Suddenly I found myself speaking on behalf of Tatars exiled from the Crimea, Pentecostals persecuted for teaching religion to their children, Lithuanian priests, Armenian nationalists and many others." These long-standing strands of repression had not had the reach and resources of the emigration protests until the Helsinki Accords brought them together as combined aspects of Basket Three compliance.

In the Western perspective, a distinction between the Jewish emigration movement, with its supporters abroad, and the democracy activists could not be understood. It was all too remote. But outside Moscow, and in Poland and Czechoslovakia in particular, ripples of Helsinki were felt, as monitoring groups comparable in some respects to the one in Moscow were soon created as well.

In Poland, where the Catholic Church represented an undefeatable opponent to communism, worker groups and intellectuals in major cities organized protests against government policies that deployed the Helsinki provisions as justification for their demands. In Czechoslovakia, the organizing group was called Charter 77; among its founders were the playwright Václav Havel and others who would go on to lead the country after the collapse of communism in 1989.

From the outside, the Warsaw Pact appeared to be a monolith dominated by the Soviets, but each country followed its own dynamic. In Hungary, the regime's tacit pact with its people to keep shelves in stores full so long as the population avoided political activism minimized dissent. In Romania, Nicolae Ceaușescu used a stance of declared nationalist independence from Kremlin doctrine to enable him to exercise even tighter control on dissent in the country. In East Germany, the Berlin Wall and the Stasi kept a lid on, but the overnight collapse of the German Democratic Republic in 1989 showed how tenuous that hold really had been. In all these countries, there were individuals or small groups inspired by what was happening in Moscow and elsewhere after Helsinki; being aware that human rights guarantees had been made, they demanded they be respected, knowing that the odds were long and the risks great.

The Moscow group began to compile meticulous reports on abuses based on information gleaned from sources around the country. Sharansky writes: "Our group published more than twenty documents. The reports detailed the Soviet empire's constant assaults on human rights." Publicizing these reports around the world was essential. Western correspondents would write about them, as dissent in the Soviet Union was an irresistible topic, especially compared to so many other political subjects at the time. It was very easy to access and sure to get attention when it appeared. Because American journalists were able to use the mailing services of the US embassy, sending out the full texts was straightforward and not really outside standard reporting techniques.

Other material was given to Western visitors or delegations to be smuggled out of the country. A melodramatic aura developed that made interactions among the dissidents, correspondents, and the people carrying the material seem illicit and subversive. As time went on, this enabled the KGB and the party leadership to use the Helsinki-related activity as a pretext for harassment, arrest, exile, and imprisonment. It was also used to put pressure on the Western journalists who covered the dissidents.

A half century later, it can be said that the information pipeline to the West probably exaggerated the true role and importance of dissent in the 1970s, and yet in the ideological tug-of-war during the Cold War, highlighting any opposition to the Kremlin was a useful technique. The overwhelming consensus in the West was critical of the Soviets. Wherever there were signs of unrest—a demonstration in Moscow's Pushkin Square, for example, or students and intellectuals in Poland signing petitions—the hypersensitive official response added to their impact. High-level Communist Party circles in the USSR and elsewhere in the bloc arrayed their propaganda resources and harassment of the dissidents, which made them seem even more impressive.

I can personally attest to the exaggerated level of concern about the dissident activity in Moscow, particularly after Jimmy Carter became president in January 1977. Carter made human rights a priority and declared so in a public letter of support to Andrei Sakharov. So, on March 21, 1977, the Politburo of the USSR met for the specific purpose of deciding how to deal with the problem of dissent, and three names were central to their deliberations on that occasion: Sharansky (by then already under arrest, to be charged with treason); Joseph Presel, the American diplomat whose responsibilities were to maintain contact with the dissidents; and me, the *Washington Post*'s Moscow correspondent.

The deliberations were recorded in a lengthy "top secret" document signed by Yuri Andropov, then the head of the KGB. They confirmed the treason charges against Sharansky and essentially decided on *disaccreditatsia* of Presel and me. This meant harassment and media attacks, but fell short of expulsion or arrest because of the expectation of retaliation by the United States, which was considered more trouble than it was worth. Decades later, I still am startled by the fact that the men who controlled the USSR convened a meeting where their focus was what to do with me, simply because of the stories I was writing for the *Washington Post* and my contacts in Moscow.

I have the document because in the first years after the fall of the Soviet Union, Politburo files were accessible and a friend, the *Newsweek* correspondent Fred Coleman, uncovered the report and sent it to me. In its way, this is as close as it is possible to get at what was happening at the higher reaches of the Kremlin in response to Helsinki-related issues. While in reality the monitoring group and related dissent was no threat to the Soviets, it was certainly a source of concern, perhaps because the Carter administration had elevated the issue as an ideological tool.

By March 1977, the Helsinki Monitoring Group, barely more than a year after its formation, had been effectively demolished. Orlov had been arrested in February and was eventually sentenced to seven years at a labor camp and five years of internal exile. Alexander Ginzburg, another member of the group, who had already been in labor camps three times in the 1960s, was sentenced to eight additional years. Other activists were forced to leave the country, imprisoned, and even committed to mental asylums. And in January 1980, the pillars of stature, Andrei Sakharov and Elena Bonner, were seized and sent to Gorky, where they were kept until 1986, when Mikhail Gorbachev, in a major symbolic step, "invited" them back to Moscow to resume their "patriotic activities."

A writer essentially unknown in the West, Vladimir Bukovsky, had been arrested in 1971 as a fierce critic of the use of psychiatry as punishment and repression generally; he was exchanged for Chilean communist leader Luis Corvalán in 1977. President Carter met with Bukovsky at the White House, also that March—another event like the Sakharov letter that was a major symbolic gesture, since President Ford had not received Solzhenitsyn; the comparison was more than obvious in the Kremlin.

My personal engagement with the Soviet tactics of the time involved a man I knew as Sasha Lipavsky, a doctor and a refusenik. We met at someone's home, and I was taken with his apparent charm, warm smile, and readiness to treat the ailments of others in Moscow refusenik circles. He contacted me shortly after we met and asked to meet in the courtyard of the Ukrainia Hotel, across from my apartment on Kutuzovsky Prospekt in central Moscow. He handed me a document he said he had obtained, issued by officials in the ministry of meat and milk production, which detailed the contents of sausage, a dietary staple. The meat was degraded with a variety of fillers, including sawdust. The document had all the necessary designations that confirmed its authenticity. This rare glimpse of a reality of Soviet life made a story for the *Washington Post*.

When it was picked up by the Voice of America's Russian-language service, which was jammed and yet somehow still apparently accessible, our housekeeper—for the one and only time this happened—asked my wife about it, reflecting a reaction so strong that she would acknowledge listening to VOA.

In February 1977, Lipavsky and Sharansky visited our apartment for supper. Lipavsky brought roses, an unusual gift for a Moscow winter. Our new baby son, Evan, was a focus of genial interest. A month later, Sharansky was arrested and soon thereafter *Izvestia* published a lengthy article attributed to Lipavsky that named Sharansky as a spy and me as his handler for American "special services," the CIA. A second and similar attack appeared later in the spring, part of the KGB strategy to intimidate Western journalists.

The purpose of this propaganda offensive and the rounding up of dissidents was all meant to strengthen the record ahead of the Helsinki follow-up conference scheduled for that June in Belgrade, the capital of Yugoslavia. To remind, setting a framework for accountability to Basket Three was a major point of contention in the negotiations. The Soviet bloc had resisted its inclusion until it became clear that to get the security and territorial points in Basket One, they had to concede on the follow-up.

In June, as the crackdown accelerated, I wrote a front-page article for the *Post*, declaring: "The Soviet leadership's efforts to eliminate dissent have increased substantially in 1977 with notable success, creating an ominous atmosphere of repression more pronounced in many ways than at any time in this decade." I then made a specific connection to the Belgrade conference: "The Soviets clearly felt that no internal criticism of compliance on human rights questions could be tolerated because that would appear to be weakness in an international forum—tacit acknowledgement that the Kremlin has not carried out those provisions while it insists that it has."

The Politburo's decision in March to launch the *disaccreditatsia* campaign against Joseph Presel and me eventually included attacks on present or former correspondents of the *New York Times*, *Time*, the Associated Press, *Le Monde*, and the Swedish newspaper *Daghens Nyhether.*

Natan Sharansky is likely the only surviving member of the Soviet-based mid-1970s dissidents, and I asked him to help me recreate the scene for dissidents at that time. Once their names were public, all of them lost whatever jobs they had. (The only exception in the Helsinki group was Alexander Korchak, a physicist who quit as soon as his job was threatened.) To make a living, they cobbled together tasks like editing texts or books. Sakharov and Grigorenko had pensions they did not lose. Ginzburg managed a fund set up by Solzhenitsyn for the families of political prisoners. This became the basis for accusing him of illegal financial activities.

The most prominent of the refuseniks received some clandestine financial aid from supporters who visited Moscow and met with them. Less celebrated would-be immigrants sought menial jobs despite their previous stature.

One intriguing irony of dissent was that despite the dangers and KGB harassment, for many of them there was a measure of exhilaration, the sense that they were living in a "free" world of their own making. It would take an entirely different book to fully explore the psychological framework of people prepared to challenge the mighty Soviet Union with an intent of advocating fundamental reinvention of the established order.

Given the history of repression and years of murderous purges in the Soviet era, the decision to publicly declare dissent without a plan for departure was exceptional. The strands of dissent—nationalist, religious, ethnic, and purely political—doubtless had many origins. What united them was the degree of risk and danger involved. Whatever goals the dissidents may have individually had, every one of them would be a target for Kremlin punishment, with forced exile abroad, internal exile (the classic czarist approach), imprisonment, threatened execution, forced psychiatric hospitalization, and assassination all possible.

The full contents of Basket Three covered a great many other issues: cooperation in humanitarian fields; human contacts; information; cooperation and exchanges in the field of culture; cooperation in the field of education. The inevitable caveat said: "This cooperation should take place in full respect for the principles guiding relations among participating States as set forth in the relevant document." And the Soviets defined this as "non-interference in the internal affairs" of the countries.

While the caption or catch-all for these matters became "human rights," the major focus was on the role of dissidents. This was the case in part because their activities and the retribution that resulted were so easy for observers to record. And the efforts involved with measuring the other factors in Basket Three were considerable. "Soft power," which is what these things were, involved data of many kinds that had to be collected. The harassment of dissidents, detention, trials, and overall KGB pressure were much more dramatic. The interaction between the dissidents, especially in Moscow, and the

Western media became central to the perception of Soviet-bloc compliance with the Final Act.

Probably the most extensive explanation of how the Soviet establishment regarded the dissidents was provided by Georgi Arbatov, the longtime director of the Institute for the Study of the USA and Canada. Arbatov, who died in 2010, was the author of *The System: An Insider's Life in Soviet Politics*, published by Times Books/Random House in 1992. I was the publisher of that imprint at the time and knew Arbatov well, back to his visit to Ann Arbor in 1974, while I was studying Russian there (and helped him decipher a health food restaurant menu). Arbatov was considered one of the most astute of the high-ranking Russians authorized to deal with Americans, including visitors of importance and journalists.

Arbatov had a Jewish father who was a prominent Bolshevik, but his Jewish ancestry never appeared to be a factor in his activities. He had served in the Red Army in World War II and joined the Soviet Academy of Sciences. In 1960, he was elected to the party Central Committee and was an adviser to four successive Soviet leaders, beginning with Leonid Brezhnev.

After the fall of the USSR, Arbatov was an adviser to the State Duma, which suggests he made the transition from party functionary to the new order. Arbatov retained a prominent literary agent in New York and contracted for the book. (Among high-level Russians in that period, a book contract in the West was a sign of prestige, and he was paid in dollars, a distinct asset.) The book was well received. George Kennan, the eminence in Soviet studies, wrote: "Arbatov's memoirs are highly interesting and important . . . [with] great historical value."

The book's introduction was written by Strobe Talbott, a journalist with considerable stature among Russian specialists; in his twenties he had been the translator of Nikita Khrushchev's memoirs, and he would later become deputy secretary of state in the Clinton administration. He wrote: "The pages that follow reflect a genuine intellectual odyssey, the evolution of a member of the *nomenklatura*, or ruling class, who 'for a long time . . . did not give much thought to the monstrous absurdity' of the system, but who came to recognize many of its flaws and tried to make a difference for the better."

Here is what Arbatov wrote about the dissidents, starting with the end of the Stalin era of brutal repression and purges:

> One has to admit that the new coercive measures developed in the Brezhnev years were rather ingenious. A new sociopolitical phenomenon—the dissident—was born as was a new array of measures against him: social isolation, sophisticated slander organized by experts in the field, concentrated efforts aimed at completely compromising an individual, the misuse of psychiatric wards, expulsion from the country and the revocation of citizenship, and to a limited extent, arrest and conviction . . . [and] in the long run we paid for them dearly. We paid a particularly high price in the attitudes of the world community toward the Soviet Union and its policies.
>
> This was a key component of our Cold War relationships. You can start a cold war and sustain it as the centerpiece of relations for decades under only one condition: that people believe in the existence of a fearsome enemy and, if possible, a repulsive one. The fear of the enemy has to be great enough for people to be willing to spend exorbitantly to continue an arms race, to risk war, even to waive their rights to an independent policy . . . in

the West, the popular saying, "Better Dead than Red" expressed the fear rampant at the time . . .

I did not approve of the West's efforts to organize political games around the fundamental issue of human rights . . . the campaign made it easy for our conservatives to identify the democrats, the dissidents with foreign powers—which often were very hostile to the Soviet Union . . . the campaign against the dissidents involved only a relatively small number of people. But it had a noticeable negative effect abroad and it poisoned the political atmosphere at home, worsened the already repressed circumstances in culture, in social thought, and in the attitudes of all thinking people.

They could not regard this as being anything other than a rebirth of the Stalinist practices of political persecution, intimidation and pressure, even if the methods were milder and less sweeping.

In other words, Arbatov concludes, the dissidents served a Western purpose in highlighting the evils of the Soviet and bloc systems. In the USSR itself, the repression of dissent meant that any broader discussion of reform, so essential in Arbatov's post-mortem assessment, could not happen.

IN REVISITING THE provisions of Basket Three, there were a great many that might actually have been useful to the Kremlin, had the Soviet leadership recognized the potential. From the Baltics to the Caucasus, from Ukraine to Central Asia all the way to the Chinese border, the Union of Soviet Socialist Republics was so much more a complex fabric of histories, ethnicities, religions, and temperaments than was understood in the West that some regional autonomy would have strengthened the country's unity. All those tagged as "Russians" when they were actually Estonians, Georgians, Tajiks, Armenians, and so many other nationalities might have been economic and cultural assets they could not be when the Kremlin exercised draconian control.

Skillful use of a range of issues such as family reunification, cultural exchanges, and access to popular Western magazines could have improved the national mood where passivity was so often the norm. The standard Soviet joke was "They pretend to pay me, and I pretend to work." Human nature favors enjoyment over suppression, and that means much more than unlimited quantities of vodka, the age-old Russian joy and curse. I was in Tbilisi, the capital of Georgia, in the fall of 1974 when the stars of Grand Ole Opry—led by Tennessee Ernie Ford, whose song "Sixteen Tons" was a huge global hit—disembarked from a flight that had started in Atlanta, in a very different Georgia. You can imagine the enthusiasm among the crowd at that night's concert.

The Soviets couldn't or wouldn't see past their narrow focus; to them human rights was a Western-inspired menace. Arbatov writes of the deeply embedded "inferiority complex" of Russians, offset by self-aggrandizement and belligerence. After two decades in power, Vladimir Putin has in our time embraced the classic Russian litany of defensive grievance, which sees suppression as the best means of control. Arbatov also attributes much of the post-Helsinki lassitude to what he calls Leonid Brzehnev's "disease" and the consequences of "stagnation" that began in 1975 and only worsened until his death in 1982.

Arbatov writes that Brezhnev's loss of concentration, and even his speech skills, began with what was probably a stroke (although never specifically described) during the November 1974 summit meeting with President Ford in Vladivostok. The surrounding officials and bureaucrats recognized that it was best to keep in check anything that might be risky when it came to loosening the country's policies at home. Instead, anything outside convention was seen as threatening, and the KGB's preeminence increased. This was a post-Stalinist approach, in which intimidation and censorship as well as self-censorship were more a fact than deadly purges, show trials, and brutality. The Gulag had scores of political prisoners and Siberia had exiles.

Every major "research" institution, including the USA Institute, had KGB functionaries assigned to it, under false identification; but this was widely known to be the case, assuring that all work was politicized. The consequence was to degrade their professional work and mislead the Kremlin as to the real situation in the country and abroad.

And finally, the almost total lack of civil society aside from sanctioned patriotic youth, veterans, and women's groups added to the misleading portrait of national stability and measurements of economic progress that were façades—*pokazhuka* for show, phony progress.

The Voice of America, Radio Liberty in Russian, and Radio Free Europe in the many languages of the East bloc became more important as sources of information after the Helsinki Accords because jamming was reduced. As a reporter for the *Washington Post*, I became aware that my stories and those of others in the Western press corps, a form of journalism unknown in Russia, were read back to the Russians.

"You are Osnos?" a provincial official greeted me on more than one occasion. "I thought you would be older . . ."

BEING A JOURNALIST rather than a diplomat or political scientist, I was especially interested in the role correspondents had in portraying dissent, especially after the Helsinki Accords codified rules that could be used as a measurement of compliance.

I came to believe there was an information loop that to some extent altered Soviet reality by emphasizing dissident activities and attitudes. This could turn the work of correspondents, inadvertently, into something well short of propaganda but with a narrower perspective on what was happening in the country than might otherwise have been the case. As I wrote earlier, the vastness and complexity of Soviet society, reflected in lifestyle choices and cultures from the Arctic to the Crimea and to the Muslim hinterlands of Central Asia, tended to be obscured in Western reporting.

The Kremlin and the KGB were also responsible for that fact, of course, by restricting the ability of reporters to travel readily and by keeping a careful watch on what they might find out on those travels, when they were invariably closely surveilled. Moreover, the pretense that journalists were to one degree or another representative of hostile foreign influence made journalism seem ideologically inspired. When the system portrays itself in glowing terms and any responsible reporter sees the flaws and records them, the result is to highlight the contrast. Subtlety and nuance were not typical in writing about the Soviets or in their responses.

One aspect of this affinity between the journalists and the dissidents, particularly those wishing to emigrate and willing to openly challenge Soviet authority, made me uneasy. Barbara Walker, a professor at the University of Nevada, Las Vegas, identified this factor in a 2012 paper called "The Moscow Correspondents, Soviet Human Rights Activists, and the

Problem of the Western Gift." Walker writes that the support journalists provided the dissidents could mean "life-saving publicity for certain political prisoners; transportation of letters, documents and manuscripts whether directly or to personnel of the American embassy," where reporters had access to the embassy's postal service. In addition, reporters were asked for and often gave Western consumer goods and medicine to their dissident friends. Walker quotes me as telling her that my wife and I were aware of and made uncomfortable by what I called *malenkaya prozhbas*, "small requests" that were a quid pro quo in these relationships. Reluctance to accommodate these requests, especially when they went beyond goods to what amounted to virtual advocacy of dissident plight, could elicit negative reactions that made reporting more difficult. The need for medicines was pervasive, and that never posed a problem. In one instance we carried X-rays to London, where a specialist was able to diagnose a serious issue.

Many dissidents were our friends. We admired their courage. Thinking about it now, I recognize an unbridgeable gap. They knew we were safe and would leave. They were not.

Bear in mind, also, that reporters had to fend off the authorities, who would monitor critically what they were doing and attack them publicly, as they did to me in 1977. By nature, dissidents could also be churlish and critical. They were, after all, dissidents. Andrei Amalrik, who gained global fame and Siberian exile for his prescient book *Will the Soviet Union Survive Until 1984?* (released in 1970), published a letter in the *New York Review of Books* in 1971 intended to humiliate American reporters for their cowardice in their coverage of the country. Amalrik appended a note that said: "The name of [one] well-known correspondent for a Western news agency is known to the editors but has been omitted here."

In Moscow, the names of the reporters being assailed were widely shared.

After his exile, when we were invited to his home, Amalrik's noticeably boorish treatment of his wife led mine to say that we would not return the invitation. In time, Amalrik solicited other dissidents to sign a letter denouncing me for inattention. Fortunately, no one joined him and the prospect faded, but I did sense that my standing among some dissidents was slightly tarnished.

At the end of our tour in 1977, I wrote an article for the *Columbia Journalism Review* on the topic of the interaction between correspondents and their dissident friends and sources. Rather than summarize my analysis here in self-approving fashion, this is how that piece was portrayed in the book *Cold War Correspondents: Soviet and American Reporters on the Ideological Frontiers* by Dina Fainberg, a professor of modern history at City, University of London:

She notes that I acknowledged it was difficult "to be completely objective or critical about dissidents" because we so admired their opposition to the Soviets and needed them to help us write stories about life and times in the country. And yet, she quotes me as writing: "Dissidents in the Soviet Union say what most Americans want—and expect to hear about the evils of communism. Excessive dependence on them, however, creates a picture . . . that is as oversimplified in a way as Soviet reports about the United States being a land of little more than poverty, violence, corruption, and racism."

Fainberg concludes: "Osnos's reflections were outstanding both in their irreverent attitude toward American reporting on Soviet dissent and in their willingness to interrogate the very pillars of his colleagues' personal and professional self-understanding." Fainberg adds, however, that my observations had no discernible impact on discussion of the subject.

T HE SOVIET "CRACKDOWN" of 1977 was meant to culminate with the Belgrade follow-up to Helsinki, scheduled for that June. Ambassador Sherer, my father-in-law, who had led the US delegation to the Final Act, was named to lead the delegation for this phase also. In Moscow, Susan and I debated whether to alert him about the stepped-up harassment of correspondents, including me, when working conditions for journalists was a core issue in the review of compliance with the accords.

Warning signs of possible trouble for me were clear. A plan to drive across the Finnish border on the way to Helsinki to trade our Volvo for a new one was adjusted when Regina Kozakova, our office manager and translator, told me (in an outdoor conversation to avoid any bugging devices) that I should not go. Later, in 2019, she told me that her judgment was based on the general atmosphere at the time rather than on specific questioning of her by the KGB, which oversaw the agency that provided translators for Western reporters. Regina said she had suspected that at the Soviet side of the Finnish border, a search of the car would turn up either prohibited literature or drugs. Instead, Susan was accompanied by a diplomatic wife on the trip, and it went off uneventfully.

So we placed a call to Ambassador Sherer on the assumption that his phone and ours were being monitored and suggested he tell his Soviet counterpart that his son-in-law was a correspondent in Moscow and that trouble for him might complicate matters in Belgrade.

Like a water tap being turned off, our situation in Moscow changed over the next few days, although I never really knew what Ambassador Sherer had said.

Instead, days before another American reporter, Robert C. Toth of the *Los Angeles Times*, was scheduled to leave Moscow at the end of a three-year tour, he was picked up on the street in front of his apartment as he accepted an envelope of material on "parapsychology" from a "friend" who had called him. Toth was interrogated for four days in Lefortovo Prison and required to sign papers in Russian that were later used in Natan Sharansky's treason trial.

Again, we'll never know the backstory, but at the end of June we also left Moscow at the close of our scheduled time there.

This account of the role of dissent and dissenters after the 1975 Final Act (and one journalist's recollection of it) provides a glimpse, a strand, of how the scale of Basket Three, rhetorical and grandiose as its intentions were, eventually came to play a role in the cascade of events and circumstances that ended so soon thereafter in the downfall of a great empire.

FOUR

Belgrade

B ELGRADE WAS CHOSEN as the site for the follow-up
conference because it was the capital of the Socialist Federal Republic of Yugoslavia, comprised of six
South Slavic states and peoples, and also a leading member
of what were called the "Neutral and Non-Aligned" countries
in the Helsinki process. After World War II, Josip Broz Tito,
who was part Croat and part Slovene (two of the ethnic components of the Yugoslav people) and who had led the Partisans
against the Nazis, became effectively dictator of the country,
maintaining the position until he died in 1980.

Tito's stature came from his skill at maintaining a distance from the Soviets while essentially adhering to many of
communism's economic and social doctrines. And by force of
his charisma and political skills, he was a prominent figure
in world events in that era, in which countries like India and
Indonesia also straddled the East-West ideological divide.

Yugoslavia as a federated state had been in existence since
the end of World War I and was an established fact on the
global scene. Experts debated whether the country would stay
unified after Tito was gone, and a decade after his death the
country fell apart. The 1990s brought war and turmoil to the

Balkans, and the republics have thereafter remained unstable to one degree or another.

But as a setting for a 1977 conference, Belgrade was ideal. A new conference center had been completed, a venue suitable for the hundreds of diplomats, press, and observers who would gather for the start of the preparatory talks in mid-June. These talks were designed as the venue for agreeing on an agenda and the management details for the full session. The national delegations were at the same official level as they were in the Geneva negotiations, meaning they consisted of diplomats and advisers rather than high-level envoys or celebrated names.

The American delegation was again led by Ambassador Sherer, who had completed his tenure as ambassador to Czechoslovakia and had been approved by the Senate for the new post. His deputy once again was John J. Maresca (later to become the principal historian of the Helsinki deliberations). Sherer had served in Eastern Europe in various positions for a quarter century and was deeply knowledgeable about the region and the intricacies of the Final Act.

To remind, for most of the time between 1972 and the summit of August 1975, Washington's interest in the talks was so minimal that the delegation was able to develop its own approach. The message from Washington had been basically to keep the Kremlin in check by avoiding confrontation and giving the Soviets the gains they wanted on security issues while pressing for the provisions on human rights to be included. To the extent that a conference of thirty-five nations to create a template for Europe could be obscure to Americans, the Conference on Security and Cooperation in Europe was obscure.

Nonetheless, the opening of the Belgrade talks was perceived as a significant news event, and about 350 journalists were on hand, according to a comprehensive official report prepared for Congress when the sessions concluded and from which much of this chapter detail is drawn. But as the discussions turned substantive, the coverage dissipated. It was always the case that the CSCE was primarily of interest as a setting for Cold War arguments, particularly since the outcomes were agreements and not treaties that had to be ratified. And the deliberations of the conference required unanimity of all thirty-five signatories, a guarantee that the language would always be parsed rather than explicit.

At this point, I was no longer the *Washington Post*'s Moscow correspondent and was spending the summer of 1977 preparing for my new position as the newspaper's foreign editor. I could not have been closer, personally, to the delegation's leader, yet whatever discussions we had then or later gave me context and insight but a bare minimum of insider secrets or gossip.

A major development that was to shape the meetings going forward was the establishment of the US Commission on Security and Cooperation in Europe, an unusual entity in that it consisted of members of both houses of Congress and officials from the State, Defense, and Commerce Departments, along with a designated staff. The commission was ostensibly designed to deal with all aspects of the Helsinki Accords, but only the human rights aspects generated much attention. It was established at the instigation of Representative Millicent Fenwick, the New Jersey Republican who had highlighted the potential value of Basket Three's humanitarian provisions to dissidents in Moscow and their congressional allies. Bipartisan in membership, the commission reflected the broad consensus that challenging the Soviet bloc on human rights grounds and warning of the threats of Soviet military power would be enormously popular among otherwise diverse groups: national security conservatives and human rights liberals, bolstered by the organized and influential movement on Jewish immigration. It came into being at almost the same time as the creation of the Moscow monitoring group, followed by similar human rights advocacy groups in Czechoslovakia, Poland, and East Germany.

As already noted, the election of Jimmy Carter to the presidency and his deeply ingrained commitment to the broadest definition of human rights—a combination of his religious beliefs, experience as a white southerner in the civil rights era, and a humanitarian impulse that would for decades after he left the White House define his standing in America and the world—represented a major shift in US policy. But when it came to human rights issues in the Soviet bloc, Carter was probably less knowledgeable than and much influenced by his national security adviser, Zbigniew Brzezinski, a Polish émigré very attuned to the spirit of opposition in his ancestral homeland and the other countries of the region. Secretary of State Cyrus Vance was a traditional globalist and a strong advocate of democracy, but not nearly the forceful presence on human rights that Brzezinski became. Patricia Derian, the assistant secretary of state for human rights, was a passionate advocate of rights based on her background as an activist in Mississippi and her work for the American Civil Liberties Union (ACLU).

Carter's early letter to Andrei Sakharov put the Soviets on notice that the new administration regarded Helsinki and the CSCE process as a major theme in its agenda on dealing with the Kremlin. The impact of that was felt by the delegation in Belgrade where the diplomats from State had almost immediate disagreements with the politically inclined staff of the commission.

Even though the preparatory phase was largely administrative, East-West differences emerged. The Soviets wanted a specific time limit on the conference, while the West wanted it to be open ended, so that the debates would not be curtailed and the Soviets could not hold the floor on security issues in order to cut short the human rights discussion.

Malcolm W. Browne, the *New York Times* correspondent based in Belgrade, wrote of the preparatory talks under the headline "Belgrade Parley: Few Hopes." The tone of the piece came through in this summary sentence: the session was closing today, he wrote, "as much because the official interpreters are going on vacation as for any other reason." The issue of the length of the conference was resolved, Browne said, "over caviar and drinks" between Sherer and his Soviet counterpart, Yuri Vorontsov. The bonhomie was sufficient to blur "the sharpness of the dispute sufficiently that the Russians reportedly agreed to the idea of letting the full conference run without a fixed closing date." His prediction was that human rights activists would be disappointed by the outcome at Belgrade, which again reflected the view that the conference was about posturing rather than results.

The agenda as agreed did include discussion and proposals of the security and economic aspects of the accord, and committees were set up to deal with them. But for the United States, the overwhelming emphasis was going to be the Soviets' human rights record, as much an exercise in critical rhetoric as a means of making progress on détente overall.

Politics and posturing also had their effect on the US delegation in Belgrade. The White House decided to appoint a new leader: Arthur Goldberg, who had been secretary of labor in the Kennedy administration, an associate justice of the Supreme Court, and US ambassador to the United Nations, a trifecta of positions that gave him national prominence with an ego to match. Ambassador Sherer was kept on as deputy head of the delegation because, according to John Maresca, he had Senate approval and to withdraw him would have been an insult to the Foreign Service. (Maresca was summarily removed from the team and reassigned to another diplomatic post in Paris.) The rest of the US delegation consisted of all the members of the bipartisan congressional commission and six "public members" who represented business, academia, and labor.

Carroll Sherer, the estimable wife of the ambassador (and my mother-in-law), was a public delegate, along with Arthur Goldberg's wife, Dorothy. In her memoir, *A Great Adventure: Thirty Years in Diplomatic Service*, written after her husband and Goldberg had died, Carroll Sherer was blunt about her recollection of Belgrade. After Arthur Goldberg's appointment, she wrote:

> The Goldbergs had invited us for cocktails at their apartment . . . but that was the only time I saw them until Belgrade, when we were told that the little house reserved for us on embassy property had been reassigned to the Goldbergs who, regarding themselves as vulnerable, had asked that the Marine guards be stationed at all times. We had a very cozy little house also on the campus of the embassy, but we required no guards.
>
> In the end the Belgrade meeting turned out to be a disaster. The Finnish ambassador's wife said to me *sotto voce*, "Everyone is so sad." I was sorely aware of the sadness because the outcome had been largely our [the United States'] fault. It was a new experience for most of the Foreign Service officers there who were accustomed to being able to achieve their goals by means of careful

and measured diplomacy, which they knew so well how to achieve.

Unfortunately, Goldberg was grandstanding all the time, insisting on being addressed as "Justice" and inviting all his friends, including Pearl Bailey, a charming woman, and a large collection of personal acquaintances to join the delegation. Finally, the U.S. accounted for 141 delegates while the French had ten.

The Soviet delegation was thirty-five people, led by Vorontsov, a fluent English speaker capable of going from good nature to vituperation as circumstances required. The career diplomats privately admired his sophistication in attitude as distinct from the polemical edge of Goldberg and others in the US political delegation.

But, after her scathing criticism of Goldberg, Carroll's coda had a different message: "When Albert died several years later, I received a heartwarming note from the Justice written in longhand and expressing a kind of respect and sensitivity that I never suspected he possessed." Over the twenty-six years Carroll lived on after her husband's death, she maintained her lively engagement in the world around, the elegant style she had shown in all their foreign posts, and a belief that diplomacy over fulmination was the preferred option in international relations.

THE CHOICE TO turn the Helsinki process into a forum for ideological and polemical dispute on values and principles elevated public awareness of the human rights issue and at the same time assured that the topic would be politicized— inevitable, perhaps.

Because of its length and doctrinal complexity, the language of the Final Act enabled the interpretation of it according to the preference of the country advocating a position. The split came down to two of its stated principles: noninterference in the internal affairs of other countries (Principle VI) and respect for human rights and fundamental freedoms (Principle VII).

In his opening statement, Goldberg said: "The issue of human rights represents the widest gap between the ideals and practices of East and West. It is a sensitive subject on the international agenda, but one that can be dealt with in an understanding manner, and which must be discussed in order to facilitate further progress under the Final Act . . . All the more, then, we are obliged to register vigorous disapproval of repressive measures taken in any country against individuals and private groups whose activities relate solely to promoting the Final Act and promises."

Goldberg was signaling that the United States would be specifically calling out the arrests and exile of members of the Helsinki-related groups in Russia, Czechoslovakia, Poland, and East Germany. Names like Orlov, Sharansky, and Havel would be invoked, assuring their visibility in the West and notoriety in the East.

The challenge to the Soviet bloc delegates was twofold: they had to dismiss the criticism as interference in their internal affairs while at the same time finding ways to attack the Americans, in particular, for their own history of racism and repression of dissident elements, like the persecutions of the McCarthy era.

As with so many other straddles in the Helsinki process, this paradox was overcome by arguing both things at more or less the same time—repression is our prerogative but is not acceptable when we say it is not, restricting visas to some from the Soviet bloc and arresting anti-war and anti-nuclear protestors.

The Basket Three disputes rendered the other parts of the accords into less volatile consideration but made it some-what harder to find ways to expand security assurances and economic policies. But reaffirming the right of countries to change their borders, if popular will or other circumstances called for such changes, would later justify the reunification of Germany and the breakup of the Soviet Union into multiple republics less than fifteen years later. The nuance of language on this provision negotiated by Henry Kissinger and Andrei Gromyko in Geneva as the trade-off—with Germany upper-most in the bargain—was what enabled the West to accept the post-war borders of Europe without closing out the possi-bility that they might someday be peacefully changed.

From the vantage point of the twenty-first century, na-tional borders were not destined to be immutable. The breakup of Yugoslavia was an internal matter, but Russian incursions into Georgia and Ukraine, seizing territory by force, under-scored that the violent alteration of Europe's boundaries and the disputes over them that led to war were not forever ended at Helsinki. The invasion of Ukraine was precisely what Ad-olf Hitler had done in the twentieth century and what other European kings, czars, and generals had done so many times down the ages.

When the conference turned to proposals for adding to the range of security and cooperation issues beyond human rights, real progress was stymied by the required agreement for consensus. The neutral and nonaligned states and the Mediterranean states (Malta, for example) saw matters from their perspective rather than those of NATO or the Warsaw

Pact, and they actively resisted having decisions imposed on them. Various proposals were put forward—prohibiting anti-fascist groups from the East; and recognizing the rights of groups like Charter 77 in Czechoslovakia or KOR, the workers group in Poland—but none were capable of reaching consensus.

On security issues, the West favored enhanced notice of major military exercises and exchanges of military observers. The East regarded these as minor matters and favored broader topics such as preventing the expansion of political and military alliances and non-first-use of nuclear weapons.

It was acknowledged that the two years since the signing of the Helsinki Accords had been placid by European standards and tensions seemed to be minimized by the existence of the Final Act.

But again, with the clarity of hindsight, NATO's expansion to the east in the 1990s and early 2000s, following the breakup of the USSR, became a flashpoint when so many countries formerly in the Soviet bloc joined NATO, and Ukraine sought a path to do so as well. Russian president Vladimir Putin saw the presence of NATO on his borders as an existential threat so great that it was worth going to war to eliminate it. His assertions, as far back as 2007, of the security challenge to Russia from encirclement by an adversarial military alliance led to a generally worsening tone to Russia's relations with the West, in general, and with the United States, in particular.

In Belgrade there were moments when the conference seemed destined for failure because, among other things, the Soviets opposed the wording of a concluding document and the prospect of future follow-up meetings. The outcome was summarized in the congressional report as follows:

It was unlikely from the beginning that Belgrade would
end up with a concluding document which was detailed
and candid or which would contain a broad balanced
range of constructive new measures. Nevertheless, the
discussion of new proposals, while a frustrating experience for the West, was not a useless one. The positive
ideas embedded in many of these proposals—a series of
reasonable, realistic step-by-step measures to make relations between East and West more satisfactory for both
sides—are sure to emerge again at Madrid.

The agreement that compliance to the provisions in the
Final Act could be monitored, and found to be in breach, was
itself an achievement on the principle expressed by Winston
Churchill: "Meeting jaw to jaw is better than war." History
has added a second "war" to make the alliterative point.

Writing from Belgrade as the conference was nearing its
end, James Reston, then the *New York Times*'s most important
columnist, wrote, quoting Arthur Goldberg: "Most political
decisions were a 'choice' between the 'disagreeable and the
intolerable.'" But, said Goldberg, while the outcome of the
conference was "disagreeable" in its vagueness, the conference
had clarified the dispute between Moscow and the Western
democracies on human rights and they had decided to talk
about it later.

Another assessment was made by John Maresca in his revised edition of his Helsinki book:

Looking back, one can see the full irony of the different
phases of the CSCE-OSCE (Helsinki) process. President
Carter's approach of "speaking out" on human rights in
the East would have made it impossible to negotiate and

agree on something like the Helsinki Final Act, while the approach of Nixon and Kissinger, with its secretive diplomacy and its "low profile" presence in the CSCE negotiations, drew the USSR into a broad negotiating process and surely led them to assume that they would not be subjected later to public criticisms.

The net of the process, Maresca correctly observes, were "public commitments obtained through careful private negotiation, combined with the subsequent public pressures for their fulfillment, had a major effect on the evolution taking place in what was then called Eastern Europe."

And therein resides the paradox of the Helsinki Accords: they established codes of conduct that made possible challenges to them, which in turn had a powerful impact on events as they unfolded.

By 1980, however, "détente" was deemed to be over after the Soviets invaded Afghanistan at the close of 1979. The revolutionary upheavals in Iran, the tensions in South Asia and the Middle East, and the replacement of Jimmy Carter with Ronald Reagan in the White House would deepen the East-West divide before seemingly ending it a decade later.

It was after Belgrade that in New York another transforming consequence of the Final Act got underway with the creation of a group to be called Helsinki Watch, with its first office in a small suite on West Forty-second Street.

FIVE

Helsinki Watch and the Origins of Human Rights Watch

T HE ORIGINS OF what become great institutions that shape our ideas and culture are usually the result of a blend of individuals, circumstances, creativity, luck, and money. They almost always adapt from their initial concept as they evolve.

That is certainly the case with Human Rights Watch, far and away the most important global human rights and social justice organization in history. HRW is a nongovernmental organization—not a penny of its funding comes from any government. It is based in New York and for many years has been housed in that most iconic fixture on the city's skyline, the Empire State Building. It has board members and staff around the world, an annual budget of roughly $100 million, and an endowment in the neighborhood of $150 million. At last count 552 people worked there, an elite corps of human rights researchers, advocates, and fundraisers.

Its mission is the protection of human rights values. It is not a service like Doctors Without Borders or a welfare organization that provides resources to the needy. HRW investigates, highlights, and advocates, and it has become indispensable in measuring the status of civilians' life issues wherever there are people to monitor.

To provide this narrative of how Human Rights Watch came into existence, and tracing its history from the Helsinki Final Act, I have drawn on the recollections of those responsible for the founding of the organization, which inevitably diverge a bit on details but agree on the basic record of events. In the space of one generation, from the early 1970s until the 1990s, the organization grew from a small committee supporting free expression for writers and dissidents to a broad collection of Watch committees focused on regions and specific groups, such as women, children, and LGBTQ people, and issues like international criminal justice and arms transfers. The divisions, like branches of any large enterprise, have their own leaders, staff, and budgets. They are overseen by a central executive team and a board of trustees, which numbers around thirty-five people, on which I served for several terms. (I have since moved to emeritus status, an honorific without a vote on policy.) Board committees oversee development, administration, and the general scope of policy initiatives.

As a humanitarian organization, HRW has maintained a position of neutrality on purely military issues, focusing instead on war crimes and the consequences of war rather than who was responsible for the conflict itself. It has measured all countries against absolute standards of human rights, without regard to the situation of the country. No aggregation of human beings is ever without tension over personalities, funding, and priorities, and over the years there was bound to be some. But the most significant and indisputable fact about Human Rights Watch is how prominent it has become.

HRW's origins lay in the Helsinki Accords, the Final Act, and the support of dissidents in the Soviet Union and Eastern Europe. From its first iteration as the Fund for Free Expression, a spin-off from the Association of American Publishers' Freedom to Read Committee, to its full emergence as Human Rights Watch in 1988, the organization's instigator was Robert L. Bernstein. His position as chairman, CEO, and president of Random House gave cachet to the early meetings, attended by luminaries like Toni Morrison, Arthur Miller, and Kurt Vonnegut, along with prominent civil liberties and civil rights activists and philanthropic supporters whose wealth and generosity provided the essential funding for growth. Alongside Bernstein was a core of people in New York whose involvement in Helsinki Watch at its earliest stages set the process in motion: Orville Schell, Aryeh Neier, Jeri Laber, Arthur Goldberg, and McGeorge Bundy.

What could not have been understood in those early years was the role each of the founders' backgrounds would eventually play on their policy positions over the long term. Who you were—determined by race, ethnicity, religion, and gender—had more to do with your deepest beliefs than perhaps was originally recognized in what was the common commitment to human rights, social justice, and equality.

Bernstein was the head of Random House, one of the most prominent of New York's publishing companies, which in that era—before the emergence of so much competing media on cable and the internet—was a position of particular visibility and prestige in the upper echelons of the city's class structure. His political views were shaped by the events and movements of the 1960s and 1970s: the Vietnam war, civil rights, and progressive political candidates. Being Jewish (although secular on religious issues) and the grandson of a man who had sponsored the emigration of Jews desperate to leave Europe during World War II, Bernstein possessed a sensitivity to the repression of Jews and other dissidents in the Soviet bloc and a sympathy for the objectives of a still-nascent state of Israel.

Orville H. Schell Jr. was a pillar of the New York legal establishment, as president of the Bar Association and a top-tier supporter of cultural groups. Bernstein understood that Schell's stature would be a complement to his own in establishing professional bona fides and a potential network of donors.

Aryeh Neier, who as a Jewish child in Germany before World War II was sent out of harm's way to Britain via the Kindertransport, later became executive director of the American Civil Liberties Union, although he was not a lawyer himself. Neier brought expertise in the development and administration of NGOs.

Jeri Laber was a journalist who had started working part time with the Freedom to Publish Committee and was a leading innovator in the field of human rights research and investigation. Her background in Russian studies at Columbia was invaluable. She would become executive director of Helsinki Watch.

Arthur Goldberg, the former Supreme Court justice, had returned from Belgrade with the belief that an American-based Helsinki Watch–type organization would be an asset in pressuring the Soviets on human rights.

McGeorge Bundy, president of the Ford Foundation and a former national security adviser to Presidents Kennedy and Johnson, was approached by Goldberg (who had learned from

Laber about the Fund for Free Expression). Bundy contacted Bernstein, who was chairman of the fund. Laber says that until Bundy suggested it, the fund had not thought of the idea of a Helsinki Watch group. The Ford Foundation provided $400,000 in funding to establish Helsinki Watch. The origins of what became Human Rights Watch were that casual.

The Universal Declaration of Human Rights, adopted in 1948 after the devastation of World War II, was a doctrinal development, as was the Helsinki Final Act. But for these founders, the civil rights, anti-war, anti-nuclear, and women's movements were inspirations for collective action.

In fact, in the earliest days of Helsinki Watch, there was divided opinion about whether the group should be monitoring American compliance with the accords as well as the Soviets'. At least until the election of Ronald Reagan in 1980, when the definition of repressive regimes changed because of the new administration's support for autocracy in Latin America, it was the Kremlin and its allies that were the primary focus of Helsinki Watch's work.

Over the years, I came to know and appreciate Robert Bernstein, Aryeh Neier, and Jeri Laber. I worked for Bernstein at Random House, and we remained close friends thereafter. I published the memoirs of Neier and Laber at PublicAffairs, and I believe that I understand, to the degree I can, how their temperaments, skills, and egos were instrumental in establishing the culture of the organization at the outset.

Each brought great strengths of skill and character to the work. Helsinki Watch's initial—specific, if not always exact—objectives were instrumental in their ability to carry them out. A human rights organization with a vast mandate would probably have run aground in the overreach. Helsinki Watch was not, as so many organizations were, "anti-Soviet";

it was pro-human rights and democracy. That was its ideology, which in those years was not typical among NGOs along the political divide.

Bernstein, who as a book publisher had risen through the sales ranks, was at his best in calling attention to people; the most prominent of these at the outset were "SOS"— Sakharov, Orlov, and Sharansky. Bernstein had access to the press because of his position at Random House and was expert at using this pulpit. When he was refused a visa to attend the Moscow Book Fair, Bob organized a book fair in exile at the New York Public Library. His activities were regularly reported in the *New York Times*. He invited New York notables to meetings, and they came. In time, a number of these, in particular Irene Diamond, Dorothy Cullman, and George Soros, became major funders of Helsinki Watch and the Watch concept.

Aryeh Neier's presence was very different from Bernstein's. As a child in the Kindertransport, he refused to speak for a time, a form, I suspect, of maintaining extraordinary self-control. Neier's ability to use silence as a conversational tool made what he had to say all the more vivid. He was methodical and precise, whereas Bernstein was freewheeling. And Neier, who later would become the first president of George Soros's Open Society Foundation after the full development of Human Rights Watch, knew how to manage the personalities of the complex senior figures he worked with.

Jeri Laber brought a deep reserve of courage and ingenuity to the role of human rights investigator. As a recently divorced mother of three, she was not an obvious swashbuckler, as innovators so often are, which gave her a form of cover for what was daring work—traveling through the Soviet bloc meeting with dissidents and writing widely and persuasively about what she found. In a preface to her memoir, *The Courage of Strangers*, Václav Havel, by then the president of a democratic Czech Republic, wrote: "I love to remember how we collaborated at a time when we could still not imagine where our teamwork would lead." Havel noted that when Laber was arrested in Prague in October 1989, "she became one of the last foreign prisoners held for political reasons" in the communist era. For the women who followed Laber at HRW, she was an icon who had framed the work they all wanted to do, really, before anyone else had.

I barely knew Orville Schell. A patrician by bearing with impressively progressive political beliefs, he was able to help Helsinki Watch—and later Americas Watch, the first of the wave of Watch committees established in the 1980s—reach the legal community for technical assistance and financial support. Schell's two sons, Orville Jr. and Jonathan, carried the family legacy forward as writers whose prose has highlighted human rights issues for decades.

Bernstein, Neier, Laber, and Schell each brought other like-minded people into the founding group. Adrian DeWind, a lawyer in the Schell mode, became a vice-chair of Human Rights Watch. Edward Kline, an irascible businessman, was a passionate advocate on behalf of Russian dissidents in particular. And Catherine Fitzpatrick, whose Russian was flawless, joined with Laber in the emerging field of on-the-ground investigation.

In her memoir, reflecting the reality of the time, Laber portrays the role of women, initially, as underestimated. And yet, as the organization grew and expanded, women played increasingly important parts in every aspect of the work. In a new and problematic field like human rights, women, it turned out, were willing to accept jobs that paid less than they might have earned elsewhere or even what the men were being paid. As leaders of the Watch committee divisions and oversight functions, the women of HRW were pioneers and were eventually recognized as such.

In Bernstein's memoir, *Speaking Freely: My Life in Publishing and Human Rights*, he writes:

> In the early 1980s, the human rights field was still something of a cottage industry, so people who were dedicated to the issues and wanted to have challenging work tended to come into our orbit. Our early staffers were generally young, in their twenties and thirties and the majority of them were women. It's impossible to say why that was, but there were a lot of very smart, highly motivated women who found their way into jobs with us, including Jeri Laber, Cynthia Brown, and Jemera Rome, who were Latin American researchers; Holly Burkhalter, our liaison with Congress in Washington; Cathy Fitzpatrick, the Russia researcher; Dorothy Thomas, who founded our women's rights division; and Susan Osnos, who took a leadership position when she and her husband returned from the Soviet Union.

Reading this in 2022, reporting the surprising recognition that women could or would lead the human rights movement seems badly out of date. They have done so, along with men of talent and commitment.

I knew all these women who worked with Susan, and they were as fiercely dedicated and intrepid as it was possible to be in shaping a fledgling field. Having said that, Neier, who was joking, said hiring women was a plus because they were less expensive. And when Susan would leave at 5:30 p.m. to catch a train home, she felt that Aryeh considered her a part-timer. However, when Neier gave up the chairmanship of the Center for Civilians in Conflict in the 2010s, he asked Susan, as vice-chair, to take the helm.

Coming after the Belgrade conference, the start-up work of Helsinki Watch was done in the years before a second fol-low-up conference set for Madrid in 1980. By then, Helsinki Watch was established and set up an office in the Spanish capital to monitor what became three years of negotiations.

Several features of the earliest years in New York played long-term parts in the organization thereafter. Every Wednes-day, supporters (i.e., potential donors and literary luminaries) and human rights experts like Jack Greenberg of Columbia Law School (a major figure in civil rights litigation) and Al-ice Henkin of the Aspen Institute joined the small staff for presentations and discussion. One of those who attended on Wednesdays was George Soros, already a very rich man in finance and starting what became his historically vast en-gagement with rights and philanthropy. In the twenty-first century, Soros would make a $100 million challenge grant to HRW over ten years, far and away the largest donation it had ever received.

With the Ford Foundation grant in hand to cover HRW's first two years of operations, the challenge of raising funds for continuing work began. Unlike Amnesty International, which was a membership organization with funding coming from people who joined, Helsinki Watch, Americas Watch, and the other committees were never intended to be a mass organization based on small fees. Instead, larger gifts and philanthropy would provide the revenue.

In nonprofit, mission-driven organizations, raising money is essential, and for many who work in them, it is perhaps the most difficult aspect of the job. Bernstein, with a sales and publishing background, took on the role with gusto.

In his memoir, he describes a breakfast with Thornton Bradshaw of RCA, the company that had formerly owned Random House (though Bradshaw hadn't been there at the time). Bernstein knew that Bradshaw admired HRW's work, and so he quickly moved beyond the business topics they were meant to discuss and described the Watch committee concepts. Any conversation with Bernstein would veer into the passion he had developed for human rights.

Bradshaw asked what would be needed to sustain and expand the organization. Bernstein did not hesitate: $2,250,000 over three years, he said. "He thought for a moment, and the next thing out of his mouth blew me away," Bernstein recalled.

"I think I can get it for you," Bradshaw said. "I'm chairman of the board of the MacArthur Foundation. Let me see what I can do."

MacArthur gave them the grant.

Bernstein also had a range of contacts whose financial acumen had made them very rich and who were impressed with the Watch strategies. Among them were Leon Levy, whose Oppenheimer Funds were immensely profitable; Herbert and Marion Sandler, bankers whose mortgage empire was vast; and Donald Keys, whose wife, Wendy, was instrumental in what became the Human Rights Watch Film Festival. All of them were generous in many ways.

Irene Diamond, whose late husband had made a fortune, more than $300 million, in New York real estate, came to know Bernstein by attending HRW's meetings. Over lunch, Bernstein told her that "one of our most consistent concerns was our yearly overhead . . . she asked how much we would need. Not really thinking about it I came up with the figure of $30 million. To my shock, she told me she wanted to make a donation of that amount. It gave us a solid base for many years."

And that raises a point, on which my views are probably more defined than those of others familiar with the Watch committee history and with which they may disagree.

Many of the personal donors, as distinct from the foundations in the first decade of the Watch committees, were Jewish, and the impact of their donations was significant. The interest of Jews in rights of all kinds was strong in the decades following World War II, the Holocaust, and the rise of the southern protests against racial segregation. Moreover, the Jewish emigration movement in the Soviet Union was the most visible of all the dissident activities in the 1970s and 1980s. As a result, Bernstein was able to secure what over the next twenty years or so was millions of dollars from Jewish patrons—as he had from Diamond, one of New York's most imaginative philanthropists. She was also a very large supporter of the Juilliard School and supported the research that transformed AIDS from a deadly disease to a chronic one. I also came to know Dorothy and Lewis Cullman, whose money also went to enshrined cultural institutions (and Lewis's favorite, Chess in the Schools).

It was almost thirty years later, in 2009, when Bernstein, by now the chairman emeritus of HRW, published an op-ed in the *New York Times* criticizing the organization's position on Israel and the Palestinians, that the issue of Jewish money became relevant. Bernstein's criticism, and the increasingly contentious issue of Israel's occupation of Palestinian lands and the nature of all discussion about the Middle East, politicized HRW's policies. The uproar following its publication was immediate and drove a wedge through the organization.

Bernstein contended that his position was being demeaned. Most of the board thought Bernstein was becoming a rambunctious distraction. The evidence can never be conclusive, but I was told that Jewish donors who might otherwise have supported HRW were reluctant to fund the organization because of its stand on Israel-Palestine issues. A significant exception was George Soros. It was at the time of the dispute over Israel, which was probably the most contentious issue in HRW's history, that Soros made his $100 million pledge.

At the core of the controversy was the principle that was central to the Watch committees as they expanded: Is every country to be regarded equally when measured on the issues of how they treat their people and others on human rights grounds? This had not been a problem when Helsinki Watch was so focused on the totalitarian countries of the Soviet bloc. Or in the 1980s, after the launch of Americas Watch, when the despots of Central and South America were clearly deserving of retribution.

But what about open and democratic societies like Israel and, for that matter, the United States, where the politics enabled free speech and the tolerance of progressive views, as distinct from countries like Saudi Arabia, Iran, China, and Russia, where open expression was not permitted? HRW's board and senior leadership, including Kenneth Roth, who had succeeded Aryeh Neier as executive director in 1991, said that all countries were subjected to the same standards, regardless of whether they were overall open or closed societies. Therefore, Israel's documented discrimination against Palestinians and occupation of their lands were as wrong in their way as the discrimination against women in other Middle Eastern countries.

It was only in 2018, in the very last months of Bernstein's life, that he reconciled with the organization. He said that he had supported the American Civil Liberties Union, although he did not agree with every policy it had. Bernstein and his wife, Helen, were invited to HRW's annual New York gala and were applauded. No other policy issue in the history of Human Rights Watch proved to be as contentious as Israel. In 2021, HRW concluded that Israel was, by legal definition, an apartheid state. That conclusion, later also made in a report by Amnesty International and widely accepted in international discourse, was as serious a charge as a human rights organization might make short of accusing a government of genocide.

It is certainly as severe a condemnation of Israel as that made by Helsinki Watch against the Soviets during the Cold War.

THE LANDSLIDE ELECTION of Ronald Reagan, and the emerging conservative or right-wing swing in the Republican Party in 1980, set the Watch's committees on the path beyond its origins in defense of dissidents in the Eastern bloc. Jimmy Carter's elevation of human rights gave the subject visibility that lasted after he left the White House, but not in the way he might have imagined. At the State Department, Patricia Derian, the assistant secretary for human rights and democracy, had seized her mantle; by instinct and interest, she looked beyond the Soviet bloc to the policies of Central and South American autocracies and corruption there, alongside focus on the Kremlin.

The overnight switch in priorities in Washington meant that ostensibly anti-communist autocrats were now in favor. Anti-Soviet, anti-communist fervor in the Reagan administration was intense, at least as much as the Carter administration's support of dissidents and the emigration movement. However, that was matched by backing for "anti-communist" military regimes and insurgent movements in Central America—El Salvador, Nicaragua, and Honduras—and juntas in Argentina, Paraguay, and elsewhere in South America. Jeane Kirkpatrick, the intellectual force in the Reagan administration that Zbigniew Brzezinski had been in the Carter years, set the tone with assertions like this: "For all their faults, right-wing authoritarian regimes more easily accept democratic reforms than left-wing totalitarian states." As the US ambassador to the United Nations, Kirkpatrick combined this new stance: communists bad, anti-communists good, almost whatever.

At Helsinki Watch, the early question of how much to consider monitoring civil and human rights in the United States led to the early departure of David Fishlow, who had served a brief stint as executive director. He had been at the ACLU with a domestic focus. A search was conducted, following which Jeri Laber (already on the staff) became executive director in June 1979. Aryeh Neier, who had started out as a consultant to HRW while teaching at New York University, became the full-time founder of Americas Watch and the vice-chair of both groups, serving under Bernstein at Helsinki Watch and Schell at Americas Watch. The two organizations shared space and administrative services.

A word more about Laber and Neier, the unquestioned heroes of those early years. Laber had acquired her credentials as a pioneer would, more or less devising techniques as she went along. Neier, as a person who had led the ACLU and with a long record of advocacy for democratic principles, had experience in the formulation of advocacy. The two strengths, while comparable in importance, were not always completely compatible.

The origins of Human Rights Watch and its ultimate success were a function of different characteristics, talents, and styles that when blended had a power none of which might have had on their own.

Laber recalls that she first met Arthur Goldberg at an early meeting about the Helsinki review conference she attended on behalf of the Fund for Free Expression and was impressed by Goldberg's emphasis on human rights. "I gave Goldberg the impression that we were a well-functioning human rights organization, whereas in reality . . . we met once a month and listened to Bob Bernstein's concerns of the moment," which at the time were about persecution of dissidents and censorship. Laber, working with the Fund for Free Expression, had been instrumental in creating a controversial exhibit at the Moscow Book Fair, which inevitably highlighted Soviet repressive policies.

"If I hadn't impressed Goldberg with our efficacy," Laber writes, "we might never have gotten that call from the Ford Foundation about starting a Helsinki Watch. . . . In writing and talking about our origins, I always start with the call from the Ford Foundation, because it's more dramatic (and less self-serving) than my meeting in Washington with Arthur Goldberg."

In his memoir, *Taking Liberties: Four Decades in the Struggle for Rights*, Neier writes that he had initially been approached by Bernstein when Random House was in a dispute with the CIA over books written by former operatives, which revealed a great deal more about the agency than the CIA wanted. Neier appreciated Bernstein's commitment to free expression beyond the focus on rights in the Soviet bloc.

Once Americas Watch was launched, the group found itself in opposition to the Reagan administration. But on matters concerning the Soviet bloc, there was a lot more common ground, Neier writes:

> The day-to-day activities of Helsinki Watch were managed by Jeri Laber. She proved an effective advocate by writing frequently for newspapers and magazine[s] about the Russians, Poles, Czechs. And others she encountered on her frequent travels to the region who stood up to persecution. Her impressionistic articles humanized men and women with unfamiliar sounding names struggling against apparently all-powerful regimes with what seemed like little or no prospect of making headway.
>
> Thereby Jeri helped many in the West care what happened to individuals who otherwise had only a blurred collective identity as dissidents.

Perhaps because Bernstein had so much experience managing the strong wills and egos of Random House's publishing divisions, he was capable of overseeing the temperaments of those differing styles of leadership. Executive directors had latitude to choose their key staff. Laber had brought in Catherine Fitzpatrick, and Neier's first hire was Juan Mendez, an Argentinian human rights lawyer who proved indispensable in establishing the standards of research and advocacy at Americas Watch.

But based on watching Bernstein's approach for more than thirty years, I came to understand how his extraordinary blend of flexibility, stubbornness, and imagination enabled disparate personalities to operate in tandem. Bernstein's particular talent was in the promotion of causes and personalities. This was especially the case in the battle over the Reagan administration's choice of an assistant secretary of state for human rights to replace Patricia Derian.

Reagan's secretary of state was Alexander Haig, who had become celebrated in the Nixon years as an army general and a shrewd political operative who emerged from the debacle of Watergate unscathed by the scandal. His choice for the human rights position was Ernest Lefever, an ordained Christian minister and founder of the Ethics and Public Policy Center, an advocacy group that leaned sharply to the right. News reports said his selection was intended to place an "ultra-conservative" at the center of that aspect of policy.

Like Jeane Kirkpatrick, Lefever contended that "authoritarian" regimes should be regarded differently from "totalitarian" ones and that any pressure on them should be adjusted accordingly. "Friendly" (as in anti-communist) governments should be considered allies of the United States, and changes there could be achieved by "quiet diplomacy," in contrast to the denunciation and confrontation of Soviet actions within its own borders and in Eastern Europe.

At the same time, Bernstein had been introduced to an Argentinian newspaper editor named Jacobo Timerman, who had been arrested and tortured by the military junta and had a written a book for Alfred A. Knopf, one of the Random House imprints, called *Prisoner Without a Name, Cell Without a Number.* Among many others opposed to the Lefever nomination, Timerman was especially eloquent. As national editor of the *Washington Post* at the time, I was present at a lunch hosted by Katharine Graham in which Timerman, accompanying Bernstein, made an unforgettable case against the tyranny of right-wing military regimes in Central and South America. His congressional testimony opposing Lefever's appointment was a major news event. It didn't help the nomination that Lefever's brothers said he was a follower of William Shockley's pseudo-scientific assertion that "Blacks are genetically inferior."

Lefever's nomination was rejected by the Senate Foreign Relations Committee, by a vote of 13-4. Timerman's book became a national bestseller, and Americas Watch had established its bona fides, as the campaign on behalf of Sakharov-Orlov-Sharansky and other dissidents in the Soviet Union and Eastern Europe had established the reputation of Helsinki Watch.

Moreover, the concept of Americas Watch's opposition to Reagan-era policies assured that the Watch committees could not be marginalized by association with one ideology or another and stood for human rights protections the world over. In time would come the establishment of Asia Watch in 1985, Africa Watch in 1988, Middle East Watch in 1989, and the consolidation of the groups into Human Rights Watch.

What had started as a small group with a specific focus on free expression, democratic advocacy, and free emigration from the USSR had evolved, and decades later is still evolving into something much more expansive. And it began with recognition that the values and stipulations in the Helsinki Final Act were a template, an agenda, and a mandate for human rights.

The 1980 Madrid follow-up conference differed from the one in Belgrade. Yugoslavia had limited the presence of dissidents. The Madrid opening attracted dissidents of all kinds holding demonstrations and candle-lit parades, besieging the delegates and the large number of reporters on hand. The American delegation was led by Max Kampelman, a diplomat shaped in a similar mold to Arthur Goldberg, a public person and, among other things, Jewish. He was even more outspoken than Goldberg had been, meeting with dissidents, holding press conferences daily. He considered Helsinki Watch, with Laber as its head, an influential proponent of his stance.

When martial law was declared in Poland on December 13, 1981, the Western delegations condemned the action and the Soviet bloc walked out. The conference was suspended for a period of time. The end finally came in September 1983, at what was an unexpectedly tense moment in East-West relations.

The Soviets had shot down a Korean Air Lines jet over its territory on September 1, with the loss of 269 lives. The plane had strayed over Soviet territory because of a routing mistake. The presence of a US reconnaissance jet in the vicinity, and the generally fraught tone of the Cold War, brought relations to a height of tension, a very long way from the détente spirit of the Helsinki process.

World war did not result, and in another five years Reagan and Gorbachev were in the courtship that resulted in the end of Soviet-American rivalries and a new and continuing developing era in the global competition for power.

I was in Madrid for the *Washington Post* as the conference drew to a close and wrote:

> In the atmosphere of superpower vituperation created by the downing of the Korean Airlines jet, the windup of the 35-nation conference devoted to the means of improving cooperation and security in Europe had a bizarre quality. Rarely can a major diplomatic conference have turned out less the way it was supposed to.
>
> So irrelevant had the official closing document become—despite some declarations on religious freedom

and the rights of trade unions applicable to the communist East—that the harried conference secretariat did not
pass it out.

CSCE had been excoriated at the outset as an essentially
meaningless pact benefiting the Kremlin, but in time it found
a lasting place in international affairs. And yet, I wrote from
Madrid, CSCE

> maintains a distinctive place in the American diplomatic
> arsenal. It is the only international forum where the U.S.
> delegation consists of a joint commission of Congress
> and the executive branch, under staff director R. Spencer
> Oliver, churns out detailed reports on Soviet and Eastern
> European compliance (or in most cases noncompliance)
> with a series of pledges on issues such as emigration, the
> free flow of information and advance warning of military
> maneuvers. . . .
>
> Moreover, the Final Act, the Belgrade review con-
> ference that began in 1977 and the Madrid session that
> opened in 1980 have encouraged the peoples of East-
> ern Europe—Jewish "refuseniks" in the Soviet Union,
> Charter 77 members in Czechoslovakia and Solidarity
> trade union supporters in Poland—because the West
> had a vehicle for speaking directly to the Soviets on
> their behalf . . .
>
> Even out of the rubble of last week's ceremonial de-
> bacle, there remain plans for two conferences on human
> rights and human contacts for 1985–86, as well as a Euro-
> pean disarmament conference scheduled for next year . . .
>
> In other words, this diplomatic institution—as the
> Soviet-American recriminations in recent days under-

scored—is a captive of general international relations, especially between the superpowers. When the relations are bad, as of late, the conference has shown it cannot improve them. But there is also no conclusive evidence that through its major political contribution, keeping the defense of human rights in the forefront of political awareness, that the conference is making matters worse.

In 1986, there was a review conference in Vienna. By then Mikhail Gorbachev was the Soviet leader and he even proposed holding a human rights conference in Moscow. It eventually took place after the release of Soviet political prisoners and in what Laber calls "a fairly open environment."

The United States was represented by a career diplomat, Warren Zimmermann, who was forceful on human rights issues in the way a decade before the State Department could not have been.

Writing in the twenty-first century and considering all that has happened since the breakup of the Soviet Union and the dissolution of the Warsaw Pact in the early 1990s, it is notable that the Organization for Security and Cooperation in Europe remains very much in existence, based in Vienna with a staff, funding, and objectives that give it a place in international discourse.

The takeaway from the origin stories of Helsinki is that no narrative can completely capture every intricate detail of what happened on which everyone involved would agree. There is no doubt, however, that the consequences of the CSCE Accords, the Helsinki monitoring groups, and others with the same scope elsewhere in the world, including the creation of Americas Watch, have been, by any calculation, of great consequence.

SIX

Investigations and Advocacy

For the groups that were formed in response to the Helsinki Accords principles, focusing primarily on human rights and political repression, their first decade featured all the attributes of start-ups in a field that was itself yet to be defined.

The resonance of Helsinki varied from one place to another. In Moscow and the Soviet bloc, the act of monitoring and publicizing human rights abuses was considered a provocation to be suppressed. In New York, establishing an organization with those objectives, once there was funding, meant developing a framework for investigations behind what was still called the Iron Curtain and advocacy based on the findings of those clandestine probes.

Now that it has been more than forty years since the organizations were formed, their approaches are engrained: send "researchers" (as distinct from "investigators") into the field trained to report what they find, thoroughly and with complete accuracy. These findings would in turn become the basis for recommended actions put forward to government officials and media outlets as advocacy, to influence change.

Holly Cartner, a graduate of Columbia Law School who had studied and traveled in Eastern Europe, was one of those at Helsinki Watch who shaped this approach—a combination of reporting, writing, and subsequent advocacy on behalf of dissenters, activists for political change, and targets for punishment by the regimes.

In the next two chapters, Cartner, who has spent more than a year interviewing the early Helsinki Watch staff and examining the available books, articles, and reports, provides a portrait of that period and a memoir of how she and others created the crafts of on-the-ground human rights assessment—with the attendant risks to themselves and the even greater risks to those people whose efforts they sought to document and support.

THE FORMATION OF Helsinki Watch had been the direct result of the prominence of human rights that emerged at the Belgrade follow-up meetings and the continued focus of the Carter administration in supporting dissent in the Soviet bloc. The Madrid follow-up in 1980, where once again the signatories would be challenged to show how they had implemented the accords, set a goal for activity. By now, it was understood that the United States, in particular, was prepared to turn the Soviet human rights record into its focus at those sessions.

With the Ford Foundation money in hand, Helsinki Watch had resources but only a limited plan for how to use them. The group had a vision without clear guidelines on how to achieve it. There was no methodology to be followed beyond the goal of monitoring human rights violations and advocating against them. Reflecting on that period, Jeri Laber recalls: "It was the worst way to start, having a large sum of money without a plan. What the hell were we going to do with it?"

The extent to which Helsinki Watch was to deal with human rights within the United States had caused considerable confusion. In her memoir, *The Courage of Strangers*, Laber describes this approach in the organization's first press release: Helsinki Watch was "responding to the call of the Moscow Helsinki group for Helsinki committees to be established in all the countries that signed the Helsinki accords. We would work for the release of all imprisoned monitors. We would criticize the US government's shortcomings as well and thus show by example how a Helsinki committee should and could function in an open society."

The concept of balancing abuses in the Soviet bloc with what was happening in the United States inevitably was criticized by conservatives whose view was that the fledgling organization should focus only on the actions of communist governments.

Helsinki Watch chairman Robert Bernstein had contacted Aryeh Neier, who was then planning to leave his post as executive director of the American Civil Liberties Union, for organizational advice. Neier recommended David Fishlow, an ACLU lawyer, to lead Helsinki Watch.

Neier later recognized that Fishlow had been the wrong choice as executive director, and the stumble reflected the organization's need to decide clearly who, what, and where it was going to monitor. After the search for a new executive director began, the concept of a woman in the job was apparently not being considered until Laber wrote a letter applying for the job herself. She was chosen.

After the initial confusion, Bernstein, Laber, and several other early supporters, with Neier's backing, then turned their principal attention to the Soviet Union and its satellites. Once Neier joined the organization as deputy chairman to

Bernstein, the three had to develop a working partnership. In his memoir of those years, *Taking Liberties*, Neier writes of Bernstein that he had a "flair for showmanship and above all, a visible passion for the human rights cause. He identified with the victims of abuses, suffering along with them."

As the publisher of books from so great a cross-section of writers from Dr. Seuss to James Michener, John Updike, and William Styron, Bernstein knew how to devise an eye-catching marketing strategy. With Anatoly Sharansky and Yuri Orlov of the Moscow committee in prison and Andrei Sakharov in internal exile, a brochure headlined "S.O.S." (for their initials) was the way to memorably summarize the campaign for their freedom.

Bernstein's value was evident in the early meetings in Washington, when Helsinki Watch was still largely unknown. As Laber recalls: "Bob was a door opener. His position [at Random House] had resonance. People wanted contact with him; he had access." At the end of many meetings, a government official would ask Bernstein if Random House would like to see a book he or she was writing.

The press was another main focus in gaining influence. Laber and Neier produced a stream of press releases and opinion articles that gradually gained visibility and some impact. Publications like the *New York Review of Books*, the *New Republic*, and the op-ed page of the *New York Times* readily accepted pieces. In that era, anti-communism had become a coalition of national security conservatives and human rights liberals.

Laber, now the executive director, was committed but, by her own account, inexperienced in building an organization and developing an investigative strategy for work in the field.

On the other hand, she had a background in Soviet studies at Columbia, spoke Russian, and was a gifted writer.

Her first trip to the Soviet Union was in 1979, ostensibly still as an employee of the Association of American Publishers, to attend that year's book fair, where she established the connections that would work going forward. In *The Courage of Strangers*, she recounts her visit on the last day of the trip to the apartment of Andrei Sakharov and Elena Bonner. She writes that most of the people there were elderly and female: "Survivors, I thought. The vigorous men who had started the [Moscow Helsinki group]—Orlov, Sharansky, Ginzburg, Grigorenko—all were imprisoned or exiled." Based on those initial meetings, Helsinki Watch published its first report, "Thirty-Nine Who Believed," about the persecution of the Helsinki activists. In April 1980, Laber's photographs of activists would appear in *Life* magazine, and she was banned from returning to the Soviet Union.

Once she began to travel and write, Laber made strong connections with dissidents. On her 1979 trip, she also traveled to Prague, where she met members of the newly formed Charter 77 group. In Warsaw, she visited a group called KOR (the Workers Defense Committee) that decided to establish a Polish Helsinki Watch; it and other groups later merged with the Solidarity movement. A decade later, Solidarity would play a leading role in the end of the Communist regime in Poland. Laber remembers that the work "felt personal," adding: "People there were waiting to see me. It kept me motivated. Mainly intellectuals who were all of a certain age, many were Jewish, people I would have had as friends anywhere." Neier, who had been concerned about Laber's inexperience in structuring an organization, wrote in his memoir that her articles humanized men and women with unfamiliar-sounding names struggling against apparently all-powerful regimes with what seemed then little or no prospect of making headway. Thereby Jeri helped many in the West care what happened to individuals who otherwise had only a blurred collective identity as dissidents.

For his part, Neier brought other formidable skills to his role as deputy chairman in those early years. He had experience running a large and complex NGO and in fundraising. He also had a background working in an organization where factual documentation and strategic use of a legal system could produce effects. Neier prioritized meticulous, high-quality documentation of human rights abuses. He was also a visionary who could be clear about the next steps in the development of research projects. Researchers were added to the staff. Neier would roam the office and stop to chat. As one researcher remembered: "A fifteen-minute conversation with him could give you the substantive guidance to move your work forward." These were the skills that Neier would use effectively as the organization began to grow and add divisions and staff.

The paradox of Neier's personality for an inspirational leader was his speaking style. He could be silent for long stretches in a conversation, but when he started to speak he could not be interrupted. The effect was to make listeners focus in the way they might not have in a different rhythm of discourse.

Before long, Helsinki Watch had moved to larger offices in the New York Bar Building on West Forty-fourth Street, premises shared with other NGOs that had formed in response to the Carter administration and the Helsinki Accords, raising the profile of human rights. Among them were the Lawyers' Committee for Human Rights and the Committee to Protect Journalists, which over the years also became significant entities in supporting their constituencies. Even so, there was still a lack of understanding among the general public. Occasionally, callers would ask if Helsinki Watch handled any other kind of watches for repairs.

By the time the Madrid follow-up conference convened in November 1980, Helsinki Watch was sufficiently launched to become a significant part of the NGO presence there. Laber and her team organized press conferences, panel discussions, and outreach to the international press corps. Helsinki Watch could represent a broader focus on the issues than other NGOs that represented a specific or national constituency.

One unusual feature for an NGO was that Helsinki Watch worked closely with the official US delegation, which included representatives from the Helsinki Commission, with members selected from Congress, the State Department, and the public. The leader was Max Kampelman, who had served as a legislative counsel to Senator Hubert Humphrey; he was appointed to the position by President Jimmy Carter, putting a high-profile figure in charge, as he had done with Arthur Goldberg in Belgrade. When Ronald Reagan succeeded Carter as president in 1981, he retained Kampelman, who served until the conclusion. With so much of the focus on human rights, the transition from the Carter era to the hard-line anti-Soviet Reagan position was relatively straightforward.

The same would not be the case in other parts of the world. While the Reagan administration was more than prepared to find fault in the Soviet bloc, it soon became clear that it would be supportive of the autocratic right-wing regimes of Central and South America. When Reagan wanted to appoint Ernest Lefever to serve as assistant secretary of human rights, replacing Patt Derian, Helsinki Watch opposed the nomination because of Lefever's known support for the right-wing regimes in the Western Hemisphere. In his book *Taking Liberties*, Aryeh Neier writes that the opposition to Lefever, which was successful, was a major moment for the new organization. The episode showed that Helsinki Watch could have impact on a US government position with which it strongly disagreed. This was an impetus for the creation of other regional committees—Americas Watch was the first—which eventually led to the consolidation of all the divisions into Human Rights Watch in 1988.

Neier wrote that the Lefever battle was "the turning point in establishing human rights as a factor in US foreign policy and not the passing fad or even folly of the Carter administration, as it was considered in 1981 by the man who nominated Lefever and his foreign policy team."

From then on, Helsinki Watch could not be described as merely an ideologically anti-Soviet organization, but rather an NGO committed to human rights monitoring the world over.

In Madrid, however, the debates on human rights and other aspects of the Helsinki Accords focused on the signatories' records and, as had been the case in Belgrade, the United States with its allies from Helsinki Watch pressured the Soviet Union and its satellites to defend their human rights records. The Soviets, on the defensive, continued to attack the West and sought to undermine the ongoing accountability aspects of the follow-up meetings.

While other organizations present at the start of the Madrid meetings gradually departed along with most of the international media, Helsinki Watch stayed on for the full three years and, as it became more established in New York, continued to refine its techniques for investigation, advocacy, and access to the media.

The 1980s were the final years of the post–World War II era in Communist Europe, although as the Madrid conference dragged on, that was not yet foreseen. In the Soviet Union, dissidents were being arrested, harassed, and exiled. In Poland, responding to the rise of Solidarity, the regime declared martial law, in what was both an effort to hold on to weakening control and to forestall a Soviet military intervention, as had happened in Hungary in 1956 and Czechoslovakia in 1968.

In the Kremlin, Leonid Brezhnev, who had been in declining physical and mental health for years, died in November 1982. His successor, Yuri Andropov, thought to be a leader with a possible instinct for reform despite his KGB background, died a little more than a year later, followed by Konstantin Chernenko, who died a year after that. This became known as the period of stagnation and gerontocracy. Chernenko was seventy-three and doddering, whereas Ronald Reagan, more or less the same age, seemed by comparison vigorous and bold.

Throughout the Soviet bloc, crackdowns on dissenters tended to obscure full awareness of the hollowing out of these countries' economies. The processes that led to dissolution of the Soviet empire by 1991 were well along, while at Madrid the debates over accountability remained much the same as they had been in the years since the Helsinki Accords had been signed in 1975.

By the end of the Madrid sessions, with policy statements that were declaratory rather than substantive because they had to be done by consensus, Helsinki Watch had achieved a reputation for quality in its investigations and influence in its advocacy. The work of Jeri Laber and the team she was assembling (along with the work being done at Americas Watch) was impressive, and a cadre of donors beyond the Ford Foundation was enabling the expansion of the work.

In 1984, the Watch committees hired their first press director, Susan Sherer Osnos. Her family background in diplomacy in the Eastern bloc and her insight into journalism from years in Vietnam and the Soviet Union gave her an instinctive understanding of the issues and of how best to get media coverage in an environment where press outlets tended to be skeptical of information from mission-driven groups of any kind.

Laber recalls that after her extended fact-finding trips, her access to everyone in the movements across the region, her reports (for example, delivered to delegation heads in Madrid and summarized in her media appearances) made the role and repression of dissent an increasing factor in evolving events.

In conjunction with the Madrid conference, Neier and Laber believed that the Helsinki principles on human rights would be strengthened by the establishment of committees comparable to the one in New York. There were already Helsinki committees that had been organized in Norway and the Netherlands, though the Moscow committee, with so many of its members in prison or exile, could no longer function. Over time, they were able to assemble eighteen countries to meet in Bellagio, Italy, in September 1982, which established the International Helsinki Federation for Human Rights (IHF), to be based in Vienna.

Whereas the New York committee had amassed a solid funding base from individuals and foundations, many of the European-based committees only slowly took hold. What was called the Helsinki Cultural Forum was convened in Budapest in 1985. Unable to get space in a hotel, the group eventually met in the largest private apartment available. The opportunity for a session of multiple supporters and activists was, in Laber's view, the IHF's turning point. "It was in Budapest," she writes, "that the International Helsinki Federation came into its own . . . The tactics we used at the Cultural Forum—testing and pushing the limits of official tolerance—became our strategy, and we went on to use it whenever and wherever possible."

In 1987, with Mikhail Gorbachev now the general secretary of the Communist Party and his reform policies of *perestroika* and *glasnost* underway, the Soviets invited an IHF delegation to Moscow, including Helsinki Watch, which had been banned from the country for eight years. The Soviets apparently believed they could hold a human rights conference in Moscow, which would shift the international perception of the Soviet regime. That did not happen, but the Soviet delegation at that session was exposed to the reports from Soviet human rights activists able to join the session after a standoff with reluctant officials.

In New York, the Watch committees were growing and adding regional divisions—Asia, Africa, Middle East—and were considering thematic groups focused on women and children. The organization moved to large new offices on Fifth Avenue, directly across from the main building of the New York Public Library. In planning the space, Neier placed the main conference room (with a large picture window) so that it overlooked the magnificent structure across the street, for inspiration. The conference room's table had come from Random House's executive offices, an artifact from the early days that was again the centerpiece.

At the board meetings, there were animated discussions about how to increase the public visibility of the committees. While the components were gaining strength, they were essentially viewed as separate entities rather than elements of a larger whole. To some extent, that made it harder to raise money for the expenses to maintain the organization and to attract publicity for what was now a single global mission rather than several regional missions.

Not surprisingly, the directors of the founding regional committees and some of their supporters resented the concept of becoming subsidiary to a central organization to be called Human Rights Watch. Nonetheless, in 1988, a decade after the Helsinki group was founded, the name change went through, setting HRW on the path it would follow thereafter.

And as the 1980s were ending, a cascade of events were happening that would prove yet another major opportunity and challenge to the organization—the implosion of the USSR and the upending of its Communist satellites.

SEVEN

Becoming a Human Rights Professional

This chapter is Holly Cartner's first-person account of Helsinki Watch's on-the-ground efforts in its first years and as it grew into the larger organization known as Human Rights Watch.

MY BACKGROUND, WITH no family connection or previous travel, would never have predicted an interest in Eastern Europe, much less anything related to human rights. I was raised in Woodleaf, a small, unincorporated community in rural North Carolina. My father worked in a furniture factory in a neighboring town; my mother was a secretary at a local college. Outside work and school, most of their time was centered around the Southern Baptist church that we attended at least three times a week, often more.

I was bored and restless from an early age. When I discovered that a girl in our church had bought a trunk to pack for college, I informed my mother that I would also need a trunk (from the Sears catalog) and would leave Woodleaf as soon as I turned eighteen. I was eight years old at the time. I also wrote to all fifty states asking for travel information and spent many weeks studying the tourist brochures I received. I was planning my departure but didn't yet have any idea where I was going.

In February 1975, a car in which I was a passenger was hit by a drunk driver. My neck was fractured, and I ended up in a body cast for the rest of the school year. Although it was a bad time, I kept my spirits up by planning for the future. Lying in my home hospital bed, I had a lot of time to think, and I decided I needed to find an exchange program so I could go abroad just as soon as I got out of the cast. American Friends Service was an exchange program available for students in the neighboring city of Salisbury, but there were no such exchange programs for the county high schools, where I was a student. I started calling around and investigating my options; ultimately, I discovered that there was another exchange program, the International Christian Youth Exchange (ICTY), which could be set up for a county high school.

I applied to ICTY and was approved for a yearlong exchange program in West Germany. I didn't speak a word of German and had never been on a plane before, but I didn't hesitate; I arrived in West Germany on July 21, 1976, the day before my seventeenth birthday. That year would spark my lifelong interest in travel, Eastern Europe, and human rights. As part of the program, we had the opportunity to spend time in East Berlin with East German students. While the meetings were surely orchestrated and the East German students carefully selected, they showed me that there were people in the world who were critical of the West, in particular the United States, and doubted its genuine commitment to human rights. These meetings forced me to question my own assumptions and raised my awareness about the repression and restrictions on rights that were pervasive in the region.

I lived in Berlin for two years; I stayed another year after the exchange program ended because I had met my future husband, Uli Schempp. During that time I learned German, worked in an anti-authoritarian kindergarten (called a *Kinderladen*), and traveled throughout Europe. The interests I developed during the exchange year would lead me, after college, to a Fulbright scholarship to live in Romania (1981–1982) and, ultimately, after law school, to Helsinki Watch/Human Rights Watch.

Helsinki Watch, 1990–1995

It was January 1990. The flurry of East European revolutions had just taken place and, in Romania at least, the exact implications of what had transpired remained decidedly unclear. At the time, I was working in a law firm in midtown Manhattan but had been trying to figure out a way to do human rights work in Eastern Europe. When the Romanian revolution occurred, I was excited, but my second, admittedly naïve and self-centered thought was that there would be no more need for human rights work in Romania and my chances of finding a job in that field were doomed. Who would need a Romanian-speaking lawyer now? And then the phone rang. Jeri Laber was calling to ask if I would go to Bucharest to monitor the first trial related to the government's shooting of civilians during the revolution. I had been in touch with Jeri occasionally since graduating from law school in May 1987, looking for ways to work with her organization, especially on Romania. I had not been in Romania since my 1981–1982 Fulbright year, and I jumped at the chance to go back.

Bucharest was still reeling from the aftermath of the bloody overthrow and Christmas execution of the Communist dictator Nicolae Ceauşescu and his wife, Elena. The streets and sidewalks were dangerously covered in ice, which no one seemed tasked with clearing. Bullet holes were visible in many of the central buildings, and makeshift monuments had been set up in the city center to honor those who had died. There was only sporadic heat in many of the buildings and little or no light on the streets at night, just as it had been when I lived in Bucharest eight years earlier.

I was to observe the trial of four of Ceauşescu's henchmen before a special military tribunal. Although they were charged with genocide, there had been little effort to conduct a careful investigation and documentation of the evidentiary basis for the charges. The four would be found guilty and sentenced to life in prison after only a six-day trial. Three years later, however, the Romanian Supreme Court would reduce the charge to complicity to aggravated murder and the prison terms would be reduced to between ten and seventeen years.

After several days, I was joined by Aryeh Neier, the executive director of Human Rights Watch, and together we headed off to interview prominent Romanian intellectuals, members of the newly formed pro-democracy Group for Social Dialogue, leaders of the developing civil society, as well as some lawyers. During our visit, Vera Cîmpeanu, the daughter of a well-known sociologist, joined us for some of the meetings; Vera would later work with me and participate in most of the fact-finding trips I conducted for Human Rights Watch during 1990.

It was not until we were on the plane flying out of Bucharest that Aryeh asked me if I would be interested in becoming the director of a new Bucharest office. By February I had given notice at the law firm and started work at Helsinki Watch to begin preparations for my move to Bucharest, further inspired by Václav Havel's visit to the New York office on February 22, 1990. Havel, the newly elected president of Czechoslovakia, movingly recalled the support he and other dissidents had received from Helsinki Watch, and especially from Jeri, stating: "I feel that I'm here as a friend among friends . . . I know very well what you did for us, and perhaps without you, our revolution could not be." It was remarkable how a very small group of people, against all odds, could make such a difference. I felt very lucky to have an opportunity to be part of this effort.

I spent about six weeks in the New York offices trying to learn as much as possible about the organization. While I had a vague idea about the work, I knew very little about the concrete steps to conducting a fact-finding mission and representing the organization abroad. In stark contrast to the multi-week training programs for new researchers at Human Rights Watch today, there was no formal training program. Researchers were expected to figure things out on their own, and they did. I used the time in New York to talk to everyone I could, asking for recommendations regarding the organization's best reports and collecting copies to take with me. I made copies of organizational policies, human rights law, and other documents. I had no idea what I might need, but I tried to benefit from others' experience. On one occasion, Jemera Rone, the El Salvador researcher for Americas Watch, spent an hour telling me about her experience representing the organization in the field and sharing her strategies for dealing with the press. She also gave me suggestions as to how best to pack the many office supplies I needed to carry with me.

Prior to 1990, Helsinki Watch was often unable to travel at all in many Eastern European countries and certainly not able to set up offices there. The 1989 revolutions presented the organization with an exciting opportunity to be present in the field for extended periods and reflected a dramatic shift in the way Helsinki Watch did its work. The office I set up in Bucharest—a two-person field office (one director-researcher and one assistant)—and a similar office in Sofia, Bulgaria, were the first non-US-based offices for Helsinki Watch since the advocacy office it had maintained during the Madrid CSCE Conference; they were some of the first field offices for the whole of Human Rights Watch.

By 1992, in addition to Bulgaria and Romania, Helsinki Watch had added offices in Yugoslavia and Moscow and noted that "the ability to work in these countries on an extended basis has not only improved the quality of the information we are able to gather, but it has provided us with a network of contacts in these countries and given us an organizational presence there." Ultimately, over the next decades, Human Rights Watch would base more and more of its researchers in the field as close as possible to the issues they were investigating. By the time of this writing, Human Rights Watch had thirty-three regional offices and staff based in 117 cities in fifty-two countries around the world.

On March 19–20, while I was still in New York preparing for my departure, we got word that there had been a violent clash between ethnic Hungarians and Romanians in the Transylvanian town of Târgu Mureş (Marosvásárhely in Hungarian), resulting in five dead and approximately three hundred injured. We immediately decided that my first research once I arrived in Romania should focus on what had happened during the violence. I got to Bucharest about a month later and went almost immediately to Târgu Mureş with Rob Levy, at the time a senior attorney with the New York Civil Liberties Union, whom Aryeh Neier had recommended. Rob spoke Romanian and was also an excellent photographer who had traveled extensively throughout Romania photographing the countryside.

As soon as I returned from Târgu Mureş, I found an apartment and set up an office. I also quickly wrote up the findings from the fact-finding trip. In 1990 there was no internet yet, so the editing process between Bucharest and New York was much more cumbersome than it would be today. In stark contrast to the review process today, I wrote my first report on my laptop, printed it out, and faxed it to Jeri in New York. Jeri's assistant then reentered the report into the computer in New York, Jeri edited it, and it was then faxed back to me to make necessary changes. Still, the turnaround on the report was probably no more than a week.

Much of the time I spent in Romania during 1990 was devoted to documenting the evolving crises that occurred. After the Târgu Mureş report, I immediately turned my attention to documenting abuses surrounding the May 20 elections in Romania, the first multi-party elections in the country in nearly fifty years. During the lead-up to the elections, there was an atmosphere of fear and uncertainty, as well as a number of violent attacks on candidates, demonstrators, and political-party headquarters. Few of these attacks were investigated by the police.

During this period, Romania was swarming with journalists eager to report on the first post-revolution election in the country. However, in contrast to what would be expected of an HRW researcher today, I did not seek them out. When I first arrived in Romania, it was still unclear what the security situation would be for a human rights monitor, so it was decided that my identity should not be widely publicized; I could provide background information to journalists, but any quote should come from Jeri or Aryeh in New York. Today, Human Rights Watch has a reputation as a media powerhouse; researchers and directors are under constant pressure to provide input for the media for virtually every significant human rights event. As a result, the organization can have much greater impact, but the pressure on researchers to "get it right" while they are in the process of documenting the facts is often overwhelming. By contrast, when I was starting out, researchers were generally encouraged and expected to complete their research, review and analyze their findings, discuss those findings with senior staff, and develop a set of conclusions before providing that information to the media. It seems archaic in the world we live in today, where information is processed and circulated around the world with lightning speed.

The Mineriade

During the lead-up to the May elections, there were large protests in the center of Bucharest, near University Square. Students and professors were demanding that Communists be prohibited from holding office. When it became clear that the former Communist Ion Iliescu and his National Salvation Front had won the election by a landslide—Iliescu had been elected president—the opposition parties decided that the nightly protests should be disbanded. But a group of protesters refused to give up; they erected tents and camped in front of the National Theater, just around the corner from my apartment. Finally, on June 12 the government decided to evacuate the remaining protesters by force. Police tore down tents and arrested hundreds.

Uli, Vera, and I were observing the protests in the center of town when things suddenly turned violent. All around us, buses were set on fire and cars were destroyed. We were pushed along with the crowd through a narrow street toward University Square, until we were finally able to get out of the throng and back to my apartment. That night I heard gunfire. I peeked out of my window and saw what I believe were soldiers (or possibly gendarmerie units) lined up in the streets below. I thought for sure there was about to be a coup.

The next day, Iliescu called on Romania's population to come to Bucharest to protect the "democratic regime" and restore order. On June 14, an estimated ten thousand miners arrived in the capital from coal mining towns in the Jiu Valley. They were welcomed by government and army officials. For the next two days, thousands of miners roamed through the city beating up people, supposedly restoring order, and especially targeting anyone who looked like an intellectual (for example, anyone who wore glasses or had long hair or a beard) or was perceived by the miners as being an opponent of the newly elected government.

In addition to badly beating many students, the miners targeted Roma, who were viewed as nothing more than criminals. They also attacked and ransacked the headquarters of political parties that had only recently reorganized after more than forty years of Communist Party rule and had run against Iliescu in the recent elections.

Vera and I traveled around the city conducting interviews with people who had been attacked, including a visit with the student leader Marian Munteanu in the hospital. We met up with some academics from an opposition newspaper, and I ended up taking their typewriter and computer to my apartment for safekeeping, because they were afraid it would be destroyed by the miners. I had no preparation for doing research under such circumstances, but it never crossed my mind to stay in my apartment. I did have to figure things out on my own. International calls still had to be ordered in advance, and it took hours to get a line.

According to official figures, seven people were killed in the violence and an estimated 746 others were seriously injured. However, independent journalists reported a much higher number of both deaths and injuries. It was hard to clarify exactly what happened during those days. While protesters were prosecuted, no miners or government officials were ever held accountable for the crimes they committed.

It later turned out that Iliescu had likely called the miners to Bucharest to restore order and make sure that his government survived. In fact, before the miners returned to their homes, Iliescu spoke to them and thanked them for all they had done. Ironically, the miners would return to Bucharest in September 1991, this time to protest the government's policies. The miners threw Molotov cocktails at government buildings, rioted through the city, and ultimately forced the government of Petre Roman to resign.

After six months living full time in Romania, I returned to New York and was offered a full-time research position at Helsinki Watch. For the next several years, I would travel to the region three to four times a year, with each trip typically lasting about a month. I was still responsible primarily for work in Romania but gradually took responsibility for our work in Bulgaria as well.

Research on the Roma Minority

While the revolutions in Eastern Europe created amazing and exciting changes, by 1991, it was clear that not all of them would be positive. In Romania, political and economic instability combined with growing nationalist sentiment, and ethnic minorities were often the target.

There is a long history of discrimination and persecution of the Roma minority in Romania, including centuries of slavery, deportation by the pro-Nazi government during World War II, and forced settlement and assimilation of nomadic Roma by the Communist authorities. After the 1989 revolution, Roma became an increasingly frequent target of discrimination and violence.

Aryeh Neier had developed a particular interest in Roma, in part because of his childhood experience visiting a Roma encampment near the town where he lived in England, and he had encouraged me to take a closer look at the treatment of Roma in Romania. By mid-1990, the evidence was mounting of violent attacks against Roma and the utter failure of the police and government authorities to protect them or to hold perpetrators accountable for the violence.

For about a year I traveled all over Romania to conduct more than two hundred interviews with Roma who had been victims of violence. The research was challenging, and we always traveled with a Roma leader known by the villagers we needed to interview. On one occasion, I was in the field doing research jointly with Nicolae Gheorghe, a well-known Roma activist who would later become the first Contact Point for Roma and Sinti Issues in the OSCE's Office for Democratic Institutions and Human Rights. Nicolae and I had been doing research all day but decided to go to one last village where there had been a recent pogrom; a mob had attacked Roma residents reportedly after being called together by tolling church bells. As we walked into the village, we heard the church bells ring and were soon surrounded by Romanian villagers angry that we were asking questions about the attack on their Roma neighbors. Nicolae was talking calmly to the men. I focused on several of the women who were initially quite aggressive. I made direct eye contact with them, nodding and smiling until they gradually calmed down. Then I asked them about their own experiences, learning about the failure of the local police to deal with petty crimes in the village; ultimately I learned inadvertently that the reason some Roma houses had been spared was because they were located too close to Romanian houses, and attackers were afraid the Romanian houses would also catch fire.

In the summer of 1994, Jeri Laber took a much deserved sabbatical. The deputy director, Lois Whitman, had just left to set up HRW's Children's Rights division, so I was asked to serve as acting director during Jeri's sabbatical. Although it was only for three months, I was looking forward to getting back to my research, which I'd had to abandon during that time. However, when Jeri returned, she announced that she would be retiring in early 1995. When the search for Jeri's replacement got underway that spring, I did not initially apply for the position. In the end, however, I decided to apply and became the second executive director of Helsinki Watch (now called Human Rights Watch/Helsinki) on July 1, 1995. Less than two weeks later, Bosnian Serb forces would capture the town of Srebrenica, in Bosnia-Herzegovina, and systematically murder an estimated eight thousand Bosnian Muslim men and boys.

Until 1995, all of my research, academic studies, and foreign languages had been focused on Eastern and Central Europe, so I had a big learning curve as the new executive director. This was especially true for the former Yugoslavia, which dominated a lot of my time and energies during my first year. By the summer of 1995, the research staff working on the former Yugoslavia had been documenting violations of international humanitarian law (IHL) for almost four years and had amassed comprehensive details of "ethnic cleansing," "crimes of a genocidal nature," crimes against humanity, and violations of the laws of war. The staff worked to expose the systematic nature of the violations and identify the perpetrators; in an effort to support accountability efforts, we shared our research findings with the International Criminal Tribunal for the former Yugoslavia (ICTY), established by the UN in 1993, and with the Commission of Experts that preceded the tribunal.

Srebrenica

When the staff and I first got word of the fall of Srebrenica, we did not know the full extent of the atrocities, but I knew that we needed to send a research team to the region as soon as possible, to investigate. However, our researchers were exhausted and suffering from the impact of documenting the relentless horrors of the war. There was a tension between the urgency of getting people in the field and the needs of the researchers themselves. It quickly became clear that the most experienced researcher was not prepared to go to Srebrenica. At that point, I still hoped I could offer her some support—time off, perhaps an early sabbatical, or payment for counseling—to support and keep her on staff. But it was too late; she left the organization soon after. At that time, staff well-being was dealt with on an ad hoc basis, and there was no program of support or resources available to address work-related stress and trauma. While I am confident Human Rights Watch would have been willing to provide support, it was not readily available when it was most needed. Today Human Rights Watch devotes much more attention to the mental health concerns of its staff than was the case at the time.

Ultimately, we sent another researcher, with less experience but still very familiar with the region, to document the slaughter of Bosnian Muslim men and boys that took place after the international community handed over the enclave to Bosnian Serb forces. In October, we released a report titled "The Fall of Srebrenica and the Failure of U.N. Peacekeeping," which documented some of the horrors. I remember clearly how the researcher, my assistant, and I all worked late into the night to draft, edit, and format the Srebrenica report and how stunned we were by its content; the testimony of victims was almost too horrific to imagine. It was evident why the documentation work on the former Yugoslavia was so difficult and painful. But, in those days, we almost never talked about the impact on researchers of doing that work. We just pushed on.

Horrific violations continued into the fall, but peace negotiations were gaining momentum. Finally, the US-brokered Dayton Peace Agreement (or Dayton Accords) was signed on December 14, 1995, putting an end to the war in Bosnia and the mass slaughter of civilians. However, even after the peace agreement was signed, ethnically motivated killings, expulsions, and evictions continued, and few of the more than two million people displaced by the war were able to return home, although this right had been guaranteed under the accords. Ultimately, ethnic divisions in Bosnia and ongoing impunity for some of those who committed war crimes have continued to impede human rights protection.

The Helsinki division continued to document more recent violations, while also intensifying its advocacy with the international community to insist on accountability, first and foremost by arresting alleged war criminals. Senior officials in the US government had brokered an end to the war and wanted to celebrate. They did not want to talk about the ongoing threats to peace and the safety of civilians, which existed as long as war criminals remained in power. Shortly after the signing of the Dayton Peace Agreement, Richard Holbrooke reported back to a full room at the State Department about his diplomatic victory. I asked about the US government's commitment to arrest war criminals as a precondition for elections. Holbrooke was clearly irritated that anyone would ruin the celebratory mood and downplayed our concern, but there were already indications that the US government, as well as other governments, would not have the political will to ensure the speedy arrest of war criminals.

In the first years after the Dayton Accords, the vast majority of war criminals, including those already indicted by the ICTY, remained at large; the international community was reluctant to have the NATO-led Implementation Force (IFOR) make arrests, even though it had a clear mandate to do so. In those early post-war years, IFOR refused to arrest indicted war criminals it encountered and appeared to make a concerted effort not to encounter indicted persons. As a result, those with primary responsibility for the atrocities committed in Bosnia, including the indicted war criminals General Ratko Mladić and the Republika Srpska political leader Radovan Karadžić, continued to wield power long after the war ended. Their political influence further complicated the efforts of refugees and displaced persons to return to their homes, especially in areas where they represented a minority.

As part of the Dayton Accords, the OSCE was tasked to set up a human rights and election-monitoring mission and to supervise the first post-war elections in Bosnia. Its mission was initially dominated by the domestic electoral concerns of the Clinton administration, which was eager to define the Dayton Accords as a success in the months leading up to the US presidential election in November 1996. The OSCE mission downplayed or refused to publicize some human rights abuses for fear of offending abusive officials; this was to further its primary goal of organizing municipal elections as soon as possible. However, some OSCE field staff courageously monitored the human rights situation and exerted pressure on local authorities, even though they faced resistance from the regional or national OSCE leadership. It should be noted that at the time the ICTY closed on December 31, 2017, none of the 161 people indicted by the tribunal remained at large.

In June 1996, the Helsinki division published another report, "A Failure in the Making and the Dayton Process." It concluded that the parties to the Dayton Accords had refused to comply with critical components of the agreement and that the international community had failed to use the means at its disposal to force compliance, including the sixty thousand NATO troops in Bosnia, to arrest individuals suspected of war crimes. Two researchers and I traveled to Sarajevo, where we released the report at a press conference attended by international and local media. We were joined on that trip by Anita Roddick, the founder of the Body Shop, who was

supporting our newly established Sarajevo office. Some diplomats and representatives of the international community were
furious with our report. They seemed not to understand that
our report was based on two months of field research, and
that most of our findings and conclusions had been confirmed
by human rights monitors in the international organizations
themselves, not to mention that we had the strong support of
the nascent local human rights actors, including the Bosnian
Helsinki Committee.

Kosovo

The armed conflict that erupted in Kosovo in 1998 did not
come as a surprise. Slobodan Milošević, the president of the
Federal Republic of Yugoslavia (Serbia and Montenegro),
was still in power despite his responsibility for international
crimes committed during the wars in Croatia and Bosnia, and
he continued to exploit and manipulate ethnic tension in the
region for his own political gain. The Helsinki division had
documented years of discrimination and widespread police
brutality by Serbian government forces against ethnic Albanians in Kosovo and had been closely monitoring the growing armed resistance in the province with the formation of
the Kosovo Liberation Army (KLA). The first government
atrocities occurred in February and March, when special
police forces attacked three villages in the Drenica region,
known for its KLA presence, killing at least eighty-eight people, including twenty-four women and children. These killings outraged ethnic Albanians and prompted many who had
previously supported the nonviolent resistance of the Kosovar
leader Ibrahim Rugova to shift their allegiance to the KLA.

The Serbian and Yugoslav government forces began a large-scale offensive against the KLA in mid-May 1998 that continued throughout the summer. Many villages along the border with Albania were attacked with the intent of depopulating the area and preventing the KLA from receiving supplies, including arms and recruits, across that border. We had a team of researchers on the ground when two of the worst atrocities took place. On September 26, in the Drenica village of Gornje Obrinje, a family with mostly women, children, and elderly members was killed by men believed to be Serbian special police; on the same day, thirteen ethnic Albanian men were executed in nearby Golubovac by government forces. Two researchers went to the site three days after the atrocities were committed and were instrumental in helping the sole survivor from Golubovac to be relocated to safety. They also took a journalist from the *New York Times* to the sites, and that reporter's article ended up on the front page, with a striking photograph of a body in the forest, a story that resonated in Western policy circles. This was also evidence of a change in the way we did our work in the Helsinki region; while in the past we would have stayed away from areas with active fighting, by the time of the Kosovo conflict we were sending researchers into areas that were more dangerous. We were lucky that no one was physically injured from that work, but I believe that by this time the researchers were already showing signs of the emotional toll.

The armed conflict between Yugoslav government forces and the KLA, which raged in 1998, resulted in approximately two thousand deaths of ethnic Albanian civilians. A ceasefire was declared in October, and the OSCE deployed international monitors to help reduce tensions in the province. However, neither government forces nor the KLA complied with the cease-fire, and by early 1999 there were a growing number of violent attacks by both sides. Serbian special forces attacked the village of Račak on January 15, 1999, targeting civilians, torturing detainees, and summarily executing villagers; forty-five people were killed. The head of the OSCE Kosovo mission visited the site and publicly condemned the massacre, calling it a crime against humanity; in response, NATO once again threatened a military response. After peace negotiations in Rambouillet, France, broke down in February, Serbian and Yugoslav forces began full-fledged military operations on March 19; in response, NATO began bombing Yugoslavia on March 24.

Over the next seventy-eight days, Serbian and Yugoslav forces committed widespread atrocities, including summary executions and massacres; as a result of systematic "ethnic cleansing," more than eight hundred thousand people were expelled from the province and an estimated ten thousand were executed. We quickly deployed experienced researchers to Kosovo's borders with Macedonia and Albania, where the vast majority of Kosovars were crossing, as well as to Montenegro. With only minimal time to prepare for their travels, the researchers were soon in the field sending daily updates on the horrors they were hearing about from interviews with Kosovar refugees.

Over the next two months, we inadvertently developed an approach to the crisis that would become a model for Human Rights Watch emergency responses going forward. Throughout the crisis, researchers worked long days in the field, interviewing victims and witnesses of atrocities. They then drafted their findings, at times in rough form, and sent them to us by late evening their time, late afternoon New York time. Fred Abrahams, the researcher responsible for Kosovo, and I would then review the draft and often call the responsible researcher to discuss the findings and clarify any questions. I would then edit the information and, assuming we felt confident about our conclusions, send it for a legal review and then straight to the communications team for release.

While, in the past, researchers would have weeks or even months to conduct their investigations, analyze their findings, and write their reports, during the Kosovo crisis the time frame for our work suddenly changed. We began to operate more like investigative journalists than traditional human rights researchers, preparing ongoing news called a "Human Rights Flash" based on that day's research: fifty-one of them during the seventy-eight-day bombing campaign.

We were under extreme pressure to release something new regularly and, if possible, daily. I remember members of HRW's communications staff standing outside my office waiting for me to read a draft press release that had just come in, anxious to know what we would be releasing new that evening. Maybe it makes sense that the communications staff would stress the need for a constant flow of information over the need for the careful fact-checking of our findings. I felt enormous pressure to get the facts right and was very aware of the damage that could be caused by a mistake; but at that time it felt lonely being the one to decide not to release our latest research. No one got excited about that decision; no one got rewarded for it.

The Helsinki division's work on Kosovo in 1999 was, up to that time, the largest ever emergency response to a crisis that Human Rights Watch had mounted. And it is work we can be proud of: we exposed the atrocities committed during the conflict and our conclusions stood up when we later returned to Kosovo to verify the accounts we had received from refugees. What is more, although the vast majority of war crimes in Kosovo were committed by Serbian and Yugoslav forces, we documented the violations of IHL and human rights law by all sides, without regard to the identity of the perpetrators or the victims. We investigated KLA violations, including IHL violations committed during the war, as well as revenge killings, beatings, and other abuses committed in the aftermath of the conflict against ethnic Serbs, Roma, and ethnic Albanians considered political opponents of the KLA. We also monitored NATO's conduct of the bombing campaign against Serbia, producing a report on civilian casualties and condemning NATO's use of cluster bombs. As was the case during the wars in Croatia and Bosnia, we worked closely with the ICTY, and our documentation helped form the basis for five of the six incidents covered by the ICTY's indictment against Slobodan Milošević. In fact, in 2002, Fred Abrahams would testify at the ICTY's war crimes trial of the Serbian leader, and later in the trials of five other Serbian and Yugoslav leaders. Human Rights Watch has also been a supporter of the Kosovo Special Court, based in The Hague, which is looking at alleged crimes by the KLA leadership.

I have focused my account on the former Yugoslavia because of the severity and systematic nature of the crimes committed there, as well as the fact that the response mounted by the Helsinki division was a significant moment in the evolution of Human Rights Watch. It should be noted, however, that the Helsinki division was also working intensely on many other appalling human rights situations at the time. For example, the First Chechen War took place from late 1994 to 1996, with grave violations of IHL that resulted in thousands of civilian casualties, torture, and inhumane treatment of Chechens held in detention by Russian forces, and hundreds of thousands of displaced persons. The Second Chechen War started in August 1999 and would continue for a decade. The human rights situation in Central Asia remained dire, and in some countries it deteriorated even further during this period. With field offices in Tajikistan and Uzbekistan, supplemented by multiple advocacy trips by senior staff, we sought to intensify our work in Central Asia and raise greater awareness of the severity of violations at a time when the region was gaining in geopolitical importance.

Although the Helsinki division had expanded its advocacy targets since its earliest years, including an increased focus on the United Nations and the European Union, the OSCE continued to be a useful and regular interlocutor. As already noted, the OSCE had large and active missions in the former Yugoslavia, including missions established as part of the post-war structure in Bosnia and Kosovo. In fact, those missions remain in place today; as of 2021, the OSCE Mission to Bosnia and Herzegovina had eight field offices in addition to its headquarters in Sarajevo and approximately 314 staff. Similarly, in 2021, the OSCE Mission in Kosovo had approximately 490 staff working in a network of regional offices. The OSCE also has a significant institutional presence in each of the Central Asian countries, with varying levels of programming. The mandate of the OSCE Special Monitoring Mission to Ukraine, which was established in March 2014, as well as the twenty-three-year Project Coordinator in Ukraine, were forced to close operations this year due to opposition by the Russian Federation. However, the OSCE has remained active in the war in Ukraine, including establishing two commissions of experts under the Moscow Mechanism that have documented violations of human rights and humanitarian law during the conflict.

IN MID-2010, I decided to leave Human Rights Watch. My motivation was primarily personal. I had two young children, and my father was dying; I needed more time and energy to devote to them. I was also burned out. The work had often been intense, and it could also be frustrating. I wasn't frustrated by the advocacy work with abusive governments; I never expected to change the hearts and minds of officials from Uzbekistan, Turkmenistan, Turkey, Russia, or other countries like them. But I did expect more from the European and American diplomats and government officials I encountered; it was exasperating that they acknowledged the importance of respect for human rights, at least in a vague, theoretical way, but were prepared to tolerate and justify their governments' inaction in the face of violations. There were a few wonderful exceptions, diplomats who went above and beyond the call of duty to stand up for human rights and the domestic defenders who were often at risk, but the majority were indifferent bureaucrats.

I also knew that Human Rights Watch was poised for another large expansion of its staff and presence around the world following the $100 million Soros grant that had recently been announced. Although there was always more important work that the organization could take on as it grew, I was spending more and more time on internal management, funding, and staffing issues and less of my time on research, advocacy, and travel to the field. I had always loved being a researcher, but it seemed that every year I was further removed from doing what I loved most.

And yet it was a very hard decision to make, and I have often wondered if it was the right one, at least professionally. The nature of the research and advocacy work were never what motivated me to leave HRW, quite the opposite. I felt fortunate to be working on issues that were so important—in many cases matters of life and death—for so many people. I also felt very lucky to work with the amazing people in the Europe and Central Asia division, including in particular the two deputy directors, Rachel Denber and Benjamin Ward, and greatly admired many other colleagues within the organization.

I was and continue to be inspired by the courage of frontline human rights activists. Just as in the earliest days of Helsinki Watch, when the Moscow Helsinki Group called for a network of Helsinki committees, it was the human rights defenders and other victims who remained the greatest motivation. There are many examples of defenders whose dedication and courage inspired me; I remember attending a trial in southeast Turkey of activists being prosecuted for their peaceful human rights work. Afterward, an elderly woman I had never met took me aside. She tearfully thanked me for traveling so far to support the defendants, one of whom was her son; she gave me a pair of socks she had knitted as a token of her thanks and asked me to remember her. She could not possibly have understood how happy I was to be there with her; there was nowhere else I would have wanted to be and no other work I wanted to do. And to this day, it is that work and those faces that I miss most.

EIGHT

Human Rights Watch: What It Has Become

THE HUMAN RIGHTS Watch *World Report 2022*, covering events in 2021, is a 656-page book published by Seven Stories Press, priced in bookstores at $40. It is austere in design, leaving no doubt about the importance of the organization's mission and strength of purpose as it rigorously examines the countries of the world, from Algeria to Zimbabwe. The report's opening declaration speaks to these ideals:

> Human Rights Watch is an independent, international organization that works as part of a vibrant movement to uphold human dignity and advance the cause of human rights for all.
>
> Human Rights Watch began in 1978 with the founding of its Europe and Central Asia division (then known as Helsinki Watch). Today it also includes divisions covering Africa, the Americas, Asia, Europe and Central Asia, the Middle East and North Africa and the United States. There are thematic divisions or programs on

arms, business and human rights, children's rights, crisis and conflict, disability rights, the environment and human rights, international justice, lesbian, gay, bisexual, and transgender rights; refugee rights; and women's rights . . .

Human Rights Watch is an independent, non-governmental organization, supported by contributions and foundations worldwide. It accepts no government funds, directly or indirectly.

The *World Report 2022* can also be downloaded free as a PDF from the organization's website. My guess is that the print books will become artifacts, on library shelves alongside others dating back decades. The PDF, on the other hand, will reside for all time mainly on screens, a safe place but not the authoritative codex of centuries past.

Far more likely to be widely read is the Human Rights Watch Annual Report for 2021, a twenty-five-page promotional PDF for the general public with multiple donation solicitations, beautifully designed featuring photography and extensive graphics, clearly intended to be as elegant and selling as it is informative.

This type of digital presentation is appropriate to today's marketing style compared to the analog book, which still looks somewhat as if it had been produced on a desktop and represents a tradition of emphasizing indisputable facts over dramatic imagery.

Times change, and Human Rights Watch has necessarily changed with them. It is now a multimedia enterprise with a large team of communications specialists on all platforms and a development department of size and influence greater, it is fair to conclude, than any one of the organization's many research and advocacy divisions.

Here is the portrait of Human Rights Watch in numbers contained in the 2021 annual report, a measure of the scale it has achieved. And to remind, in 1978 the founding paid staff was plus or minus three.

Staff: 552
Nationalities: 89
Registered offices worldwide: 33
Revenue from 22 countries
Annual budget: $97 million
Research covering: 100 countries
Publications: 6,000
Website visits: 32 million
Social media followers: 12 million
Media mentions: 300,000, in 60 languages and
        190 countries

As an emeritus member of the board of directors, I am sent the material for every quarterly meeting of the trustees and senior staff. These are confidential and cover finance and budget; a breakdown of DEI (diversity, equity, and inclusion) progress and reports from committees on policy, investment, development, nominations; and the Executive Director's Report from Kenneth Roth, who retired in August 2022 after thirty years (and a few more as deputy to Aryeh Neier), a measure of his tremendous role in what Human Rights Watch has become.

When his retirement was announced in May of that year, Roth was interviewed by Jonathan Tepperman of the *Octavian*

Report, and this is what he said about his long-term strategy for running the organization:

> I had always tried to run Human Rights Watch with an intense focus on impact. It's not enough to stand for the right things; anybody can do that. Our task is to change governments, to change their behavior, to stop abuses. And that requires playing power politics: figuring out what a particular government cares about and how to deprive it of that until they change.
>
> The first step is always to do an investigation. We are all about deploying facts and facts are powerful if you can get them into the public domain. . . . It's a process of shaming and figuring out what audience a particular government cares about most . . . we're not just a bunch of do-gooders who stand for the right thing. We play hardball and try to force governments to change.

After Roth's presentation on his activities (he was received at the highest political levels in most places and was a luminary at international conferences like Davos) and updates from various programs and departments, the quarterly meeting convenes in executive session, which does not include the emeritus board and where sensitive matters are discussed; these include salaries and annual reviews and issues of internal management. Also discussed are the disputes that inevitably roil any collection of people, especially those who choose to work in a human rights NGO as opposed to a place where the material rewards are much greater and the metrics of success easier to determine. The board has thirty-five members, who serve as long as twelve years, unless given a rare extension.

Becoming emeritus is considered a distinction and not all board members are chosen.

As someone who has been an observer or participant in the activities of the organization from its earliest days, I can report that the scale of its growth and the magnitude of its achievement is (to deploy an overused term correctly) awesome. When the thirty-five nations gathered in Helsinki on July 31–August 1, 1975, to sign the Final Act, no one, even those now in the pantheon of human rights greats such as Andrei Sakharov or Václav Havel, could have imagined what the Moscow Helsinki Group or Charter 77 in Czechoslovakia and others would initiate in a matter of years.

Among HRW's more visible achievements was recognition in the 1997 Nobel Peace Prize, as part of a coalition advocating for the end of land mines. The organization has had a major influence on international justice forums, war crimes tribunals in the former Yugoslavia and Rwanda, and the establishment of the International Criminal Court (ICC), which is still defining its reach and authority. (The United States has never ratified the treaty establishing the ICC.) Over time, the organization's work on issues has expanded well beyond the realm of civil and political rights into economic and social rights. Human rights in the twenty-first century encompasses aspects of life such as the rights of the disabled and gender identity issues, which in times past were rarely considered.

Human Rights Watch devised the means of researching and assessing human rights violations with a degree of precision unparalleled in the history of investigations. The ability to innovate meant that it was able to adapt to all the ways regimes and autocracies sought to cover up their activities. HRW's legal and fact-checking protocols set standards so high that rarely—very rarely—was its reporting shown to be wrong.

The world's major media organizations came to rely on Human Rights Watch as a primary source of indisputable reporting, whereas the work of advocacy organizations in the past was thought to be too ideologically committed to be reliable. In the nongovernmental sector of the world order, HRW is a mighty force.

This book has focused on the first decades of the organization: its origins, founders, and early staff, the people who in fundamental ways shaped its strategies and methods, the combination of impeccable investigation and its consequential capacity to "name and shame" wrongdoers. Those were the years in which Human Rights Watch was most directly associated with the CSCE-Helsinki process.

As its size and global reach grew, the Helsinki connection became less important at Human Rights Watch, and the ambitions of the organization became increasingly global. What had started in Europe now encompassed all regions of the world. Because the first international Helsinki group was based in New York, its support base was almost exclusively American. Over time, HRW has become an organization with staff, funding, and a board of directors that represents the world, and that scale inevitably has transformed its culture.

What started as a small a group of "liberal" activists and dissidents (in the parlance of that time) is now a vast enterprise that covers so many countries, political systems, and issues that its mandate is complicated yet nonetheless still based, fundamentally, on respect for the rights of all people, wherever and however they live.

MY ADMIRATION, RESPECT, and opinions about Human Rights Watch include a belief that as its influence has grown, so has its self-regard. As a great organization, HRW is now an elite institution, especially in choosing among aspirants for senior staff and the board of directors. The nature of elite status—in education, business, private clubs, and NGOs, especially when the record justifies the status—is to condescend to those less formidable in a similar line of work. It is very unusual to be powerful and to maintain humility about the work one does.

Amnesty International, founded in the United Kingdom in 1960 as a largely volunteer organization, now has about ten million dues-paying members and has expanded its brief beyond its early focus on letter writing on behalf of "prisoners of conscience," a virtuous but limited objective. Amnesty's influence is not considered comparable to Human Rights Watch's range of activities and the quality of its investigative reports. That is certainly the view expressed at HRW.

In one much discussed instance in 2016, Human Rights Watch aligned itself with the position of far-right politicians in urging the rejection of a peace agreement to end the long civil war in Colombia, on the grounds that it went too far in offering amnesty to the combatants from the left-wing revolutionary group FARC. The rest of the interested parties were chagrined at that stance, as were many on the HRW staff. After the peace treaty was rejected in a referendum, Roth was quoted by the *Nation* magazine as saying: "Looks like Colombians aren't so eager to premise 'peace' on effective impunity for FARC's and military's war crimes."

In its coverage of the topic, the *Nation* quoted Adam Isacson of the Washington Office on Latin America, who described HRW's calibrated rhetoric on the accord as "a checkmate against justice" that overwhelmed the valid arguments made by other participants.

Human Rights Watch's status and self-righteousness, the result of always finding fault in others as a matter of priorities, can make it difficult for the organization to accept its own flaws. Raising money to grow a mission often means making compromises on principles, much in the way profits in a business can undermine purpose. Despite a vetting process for donations, there have been documented cases over the years in which money was solicited from dubious and eventually discredited donors.

When a group of senior staff members wrote to the board seeking accountability for the acceptance of funding from a Saudi businessman on the condition that it not be used for LGBTQ research (which was returned only after the revelation of the episode), the signatories, one way or another, left the organization within months; two of them told me they were required to sign nondisclosure agreements about the matter.

Liesl Gerntholtz, who led HRW's Women's Rights Division and served as interim associate director, was one of those who signed the letter. At my request, and with her approval for its use, here is what she wrote to me:

> The development team often drove strategy (not a good thing), and more significantly Ken (Roth's) focus on fundraising (to give him credit, HRW doubled in size during the period I was there—the budget was around $47 million in 2008 and in 2020, when I left it was over $80 million). That focus could be disconnected from HRW's values and was deeply problematic.

For a long time while I was at HRW, we were on the wrong side of two of the most important human rights concerns of the day—climate change and technology.

Climate change: Ken blocked work on climate change as a human rights issue for a significant period because the "weather does not cause human rights violations"—that's a direct quote from him. It took significant internal advocacy and some external criticism to get the board to agree to a (very anodyne) climate change policy that was finally adopted by the board in October, 2019.

Technology: this a particularly egregious example of Ken blocking essential work because he wanted to fundraise from tech companies, particularly Facebook and Google. Ken only agreed to work in these areas when he was taken to task by two important donors (the Sandlers and Pierre Omidyar) about HRW's failure to do this work.

Roth's tenure at Human Rights Watch, and the successes for which he was doubtless responsible, made challenges to his leadership style or policies extremely rare at the board level. Because he was the undisputed head and effectively the CEO of the organization for so long, criticism of him was inevitable. Based on my many discussions over the years with other board members and staff, any critiques, even when they were justified, were dismissed or disparaged. More than once, I received telephone calls from other emeritus board members when the possibility arose that I might be outspoken in one way or another, urging me not to be.

The conclusion: the opinion of some outsiders (and several former and long-term staff I interviewed) of HRW's reputation as haughty is the organization's self-regard ascending to a fault. And the price of constant growth is high, in ways calculable with more than money.

As in any enterprise, internal dissidence is fraught when it becomes more than a nuisance. Even when the whole basis of the organization is to support dissent and disruption, the established order of internal management is defended. As elsewhere, staff unrest over DEI, salary, and working conditions, especially among younger and newer hires, requires attention, and tends to get it. HRW has a union. Complaints among junior staff are considered, even when to some of the older staff they seem more petulant than serious.

But at the higher levels of leadership and the board, obedience is expected. To return to the saga of founder Robert Bernstein's objections to HRW policy on Israel described earlier: his public objections set a standard for what was considered unacceptable when disputes move outside the lanes of polite disagreement to an opinion article in the *New York Times*.

As it happens, Israel is an especially contentious subject because the American Jewish diaspora, which was so involved in the early period at Human Rights Watch, now has conflicted feelings about the Jewish state. A threshold was crossed in 2021, when Human Rights Watch issued its major report concluding that by international legal standards, Israel was an apartheid state because of its treatment of Palestinians in the West Bank and Gaza. As far as I know, no one at HRW or its board urged any consideration of the factors that might have contributed to Israel's clearly repressive policy. For many years in international forums, Zionism was called racism. Apartheid is at least as serious an indictment.

Thomas Friedman of the *New York Times*, a three-time recipient of the Pulitzer Prize and as sophisticated an observer of Israel as there is, believes that the unresolved issue of Palestine and the treatment of the Palestinian Arabs is the ultimate threat to Israel's future as a democratic Jewish state as it approaches the seventy-fifth anniversary of its founding.

In July 2022, he wrote that the occupation of the West Bank "may not be the same as South African apartheid, but it is an ugly cousin and morally corrosive to Israel as a Jewish democracy. It is becoming so alienating to Israel's liberal friends, including the younger generation of American Jews, that if it continues, Joe Biden may be the last pro-Israel Democratic president."

I contend that flexibility in measuring circumstances and historical nuance are worth the trouble of devising such standards at HRW. Even the best of democracies cannot avoid all bias or discrimination. Every country has minority issues. The world's largest democracy, India, has never resolved its divide between Hindus and Muslims. Nordic attitudes toward immigrants of color, for instance, have been demonstrably prejudiced. The presence of people considered the "other" is a problem everywhere.

This, again, is a considered view shaped by reflection on the story of Israel, a country created out of the debris of the Holocaust. A visit to Auschwitz and the remnants of the gas chambers there can explain, if not defend, why Israelis adhere to the aggressive principle of "Never again." On the scrolls of the dead at the concentration camp are nineteen people with my last name.

An absolutist position on what is right and wrong is easier to uphold than ameliorating factors. At HRW the position is that any concession to circumstances undermines the clarity of its work and the force of its advocacy.

The acceptance of tainted Saudi money and the denunciation of Israel reflect the complexity of work in the Middle

East. But repression, injustice, inequality, sexism, racism, and violence can be found the world over. The conflicts are political, religious, and tribal. Human Rights Watch has policies that have been updated over the years—how to handle the former satellites of Eastern Europe after the implosion of the Soviet Union; or how to address the Catholic Church in Poland when it pivots from defiance in the Soviet era (when Pope John Paul II was instrumental in the downfall of Communism) to embrace the nativism of a right-wing government. Is everything that happens in a country that has emerged from autocracy going to be acceptable? Clearly not.

What makes a human rights hero? Aung San Suu Kyi, a Nobel Peace Prize recipient for her opposition to Myanmar's military regime, and once again a prisoner of the country's resurgent military, was a major disappointment when her position on the Rohingya minority in the period of partial democracy was called genocide.

In Africa, how to measure progress? Decades after the massacres of hundreds of thousands of people in the 1990s when Hutus murdered Tutsis, Rwanda is an authoritarian state that is in many ways a much better and certainly safer place to live. But it is not an open, free, or democratic society. Are there gradations of repression if the population is benefiting from improvements in their day-to-day life?

In the 1970s, I was a correspondent covering the wars in Vietnam and Cambodia. I have visited both countries since, and compared to the horrors of what people in those countries still tend to call the "American" war, they are doing well (in the broader sense). Are there human rights problems? Definitely. But I can accept what they have become much more easily than I could deal a half century ago with what they were, when the United States was at war to protect them from communism, which we perceived as a US national security threat.

Is there a variable standard for what enables people to live a better or safer life than they did?

ADVOCATING FOR AND against intervention in military conflicts on humanitarian grounds is another challenge that confronts Human Rights Watch. In the case of war, such as Russia's 2022 invasion of Ukraine, is it possible to denounce violence of all kinds when one side is defending itself and the other is intent on maximum destruction? The organization's position is to highlight abuse wherever and by whomever it finds to be responsible, through its research and reporting. This is objectivity and not neutrality, which would be harder to justify. Here is the position HRW's staff shared with the board when Russia invaded Ukraine in 2022:

HUMAN RIGHTS WATCH'S ORGANIZATIONAL POSITION ON NEUTRALITY IN ARMED CONFLICTS
February 28, 2022

On February 24, Russia's armed forces launched large-scale attacks in multiple cities throughout Ukraine, escalating dramatically, throughout the country, the war that has been grinding on for eight years in eastern Ukraine. Human Rights Watch was the first international human rights organization to seek to reduce civilian harm in armed conflict by applying international humanitarian law (IHL), or the laws of war, which apply to both state armed forces and non-state armed groups. HRW's investigating and reporting on violations by all the parties

to a conflict since the early 1980s proved crucial in gaining credibility and traction for advocacy in often highly
contentious political environments. Critical to HRW's
investigations and reporting has been its organizational
position of neutrality in armed conflicts—most basically,
not picking sides in a war or ascribing blame for starting
it—but reporting impartially on IHL violations by all
parties. This was in line with the position of major humanitarian organizations, most notably the International
Committee of the Red Cross, and was later adopted by
other human rights groups. There is an understandable
desire to cast blame for hostilities and its horrendous
costs on aggressor governments or abusive armed groups.
Prior to the 2003 US invasion of Iraq, for instance, many
staffers wanted HRW to issue a statement condemning
the expected attack. But since its first years reporting on
armed conflict, HRW considered that its most important role—its value-added—during wartime to be not its
position on the lawfulness or morality of the war itself
(*jus ad bellum*) but its investigations and reporting on the
conduct of the armed conflict (*jus in bello*).

Why Neutrality Matters

HRW's position of neutrality is a statement that that
the organization's armed conflict reporting, and advocacy will not be determined or affected by the party it
wants to "win" the war. Of course, this position has not
spared HRW criticism of its reporting—often by both
antagonists—but it has prevented critics from simply re-
jecting our research because of whom we are backing.
After the US invaded Iraq, our highly critical reporting of US military as well as Iraqi abuses put the onus

on our detractors to show how we got the facts wrong, not dismissing us because of stated biases. Over the years HRW has developed genuine expertise in investigating and analyzing wartime abuses, a field that was previously left largely to the military community. While it is hard to calculate the value of the work in reducing civilian harm during fighting, HRW's reporting and advocacy have contributed immensely to filling the public record with otherwise unreported war crimes, heightened pressure for international justice for abusers, and has pushed the development of means and methods of war that minimize civilian harm. We want to underline that HRW's position does not prohibit staff from personally expressing solidarity on social media with people in Ukraine or with those in Russia or elsewhere voicing opposition to the war or taking part in demonstrations. However, especially when a staff member's position or work links them to HRW's Ukraine and Russia research and advocacy, extra care needs to be taken to ensure that personal expressions of solidarity or support are not framed in a way that would undercut HRW's position of neutrality. Any uncertainty in this regard should be discussed with the staffer's divisional director.

Maintaining Neutrality for Staff Security

Another consideration is staff security. HRW's original conflict researcher, Jemera Rone, was adamant that HRW's neutrality in armed conflicts was important for the safety of our researchers should they come into the hands of the "wrong side." This concern is magnified by the proliferation of HRW offices around the world, such as in Moscow.

Neutrality ≠ False Equivalence of Abuses

Neutrality in armed conflicts does not mean generating a false equivalence of violations. Should a party to a conflict be overwhelmingly responsible for serious abuses, HRW's reporting should reflect that. For instance, HRW's reporting on laws-of-war violations in Myanmar's ethnic minority areas has appropriately focused on abuses by the Myanmar military, which have been far greater than those committed by the ethnic armed groups.

Consistency in HRW's Work

It should also be recognized that dispensing with organizational neutrality would raise a host of new mandate issues. Would HRW support or oppose a NATO no-fly zone in Ukraine? What about other forms of military intervention? International human rights and humanitarian law does not provide answers to these questions. But opting not to comment on such issues—whether for or against—becomes less tenable if a position has already been taken on the conflict itself. Even if one considers the current situation to be exceptional, it is important to consider how this will affect HRW's take on the many other armed conflicts we currently report on. No one thinks the civilian victims of armed conflict in Kachin State, Gaza, Tigray, or Eastern Congo are less entitled to our attention. HRW's focus on the conduct of the parties rather than the unjustness of the conflict puts civilians on an equal footing for our attention and concern, resources permitting. An approach in which we hold out the civilians of a particular place as more deserving is inconsistent with HRW's vision. Finally, focusing on IHL also does not preclude HRW from addressing broader concerns about human rights, which still apply during an armed conflict. A military force with effective control over an area must respond to protests under human rights standards, not the laws of war. Access to food and health care fall under human rights as well as humanitarian law.

Among other things, this position reflects how the organization has matured. In the earliest days of Helsinki Watch and Americas Watch, opposition to the regimes being monitored was largely ideological. The Soviet system was deplorable, and the right-wing regimes of Central and South America were in their way equally bad. Balancing criticism was the best way to avoid being labeled left- or right-wing.

Human Rights Watch's policies are now based primarily on legal judgments and standards and considerably less on the personal views and passions of the people responsible for making them. The staff at a human rights organization, first self-selected and then hired, are there presumably because of their beliefs. As HRW has become ever larger with a need for rules, procedures, and a bureaucratic structure, it has adopted the stance of adjudicator. The advocacies it is so qualified to make are stern in focus. The enormous output of multimedia that HRW produces to make, and promote, its own case has an element of paradox: everything must be based on the law and yet designed to be appealing or appalling, which is sometimes hard to reconcile.

In his interview with the *Octavian Report*, Kenneth Roth described the evolving situation in the global scene and its challenges:

There was the Cold War, when proxy forces around the world often operated very abusively with the backing of the United States or the Soviet Union ... the emergence of ethnic violence was a major challenge for many years. Then we went through what felt like the halcyon days when people thought democracy had arrived around the world. But then a growing number of autocrats began to learn how to game democracy ... and to manipulate the electoral system sufficiently to retain power without the rule of law.

Roth's approach to the changing big picture was a factor in the way Human Rights Watch became a powerful source of reporting very much like journalism—undisputed facts and judgments drawn from them. In its modern-day and always problematical best, journalism is also a gathering of the accurate, available facts from every source. But HRW does not ask for justifying comments from those it criticizes. Its criticisms are one sided, which makes the demands of accuracy, but not necessarily fairness, essential.

The last of the founding generation of HRW's dramatic growth and development—it had only two executive directors in its forty-five-year history, Aryeh Neier and Kenneth Roth—have now gone. With them goes their personal approach and style to human rights investigation and advocacy, and their firsthand experience of Helsinki Watch in its early years and of how the organization has transformed over the decades. The scale of Human Rights Watch, which has an endowment (rare among NGOs) and a record of sustained achievement, assures that it will remain a pillar of human rights.

But the future will be determined by people whose personal backgrounds and experience will shape their leadership and policies. In what is bound to happen in this long-coming generational change, Human Rights Watch will continue to evolve, as it should. Strikingly, the field of human rights investigation, reporting, and advocacy is still relatively new. That means the organization may well look different in years to come, as it looks so different now from what it was at the outset.

That the Helsinki Accords changed the world is the central thesis of this book, and what Human Rights Watch has become is a direct consequence of what was in the accords and the way they became a foundation for much of what has followed since then.

Before and after the Ukraine invasion, Vladimir Putin moved against the post-Soviet civic groups associated with human rights.

One of the most important of these was Memorial, established in 1989, which as the *Washington Post* wrote in an editorial, "blossomed into a prestigious center for research and commemoration of [Joseph] Stalin's crimes and for the defense of human rights." In 2022, Memorial was a recipient of the Nobel Peace Prize along with Ukraine's Center for Civil Liberties and the jailed Belarusian human rights activist Ales Bialiatski.

NINE

The Heirs of Helsinki in Washington and Vienna

A FULL HALF CENTURY after the Helsinki Accords negotiations began, human rights are, beyond doubt, a core issue among nations, and monitoring them is an accepted determinant of political, social, and economic activities.

And until February 2022 it was possible to assert that the security provisions of the accords, the notion that international boundaries could be changed only with the consent of the people who lived within them, had essentially prevailed. The Balkan wars were the unraveling of the former Yugoslavia (an internal affair) and Russia's incursions into Georgia and the takeover of Crimea, while serious, did not galvanize enough global opposition to stop them. In retrospect, this was a terrible mistake. The West found it hard to accept the scale of what Putin had in mind.

What became known as the Helsinki principle on borders—devised in the 1970s in anticipation that post-war Germany would one day be reunited, and how that reality should impact the division of Europe—was demolished when

Vladimir Putin launched his full-scale invasion of Ukraine with the intention of restoring the country to the Russian orbit. Belarus had already been, in effect, returned to Kremlin hegemony by political means.

Ukraine, however, was moving closer to the West and was even ready to join NATO, as other former Soviet states and satellites had done. History will determine whether NATO expansion was the deciding factor in the invasion that Putin said it was and whether earlier agreements with the West had precluded NATO extending to Russia's borders, as Putin insisted but the historical record does not support.

As far back as Henry Kissinger's 1975 meeting in Geneva with Andrei Gromyko, where the Helsinki principle on borders was devised, the history shows that what Putin, and he alone, chose to do in 2022 abrogated the understanding that cross-border aggression would not happen. The Soviet Union had agreed to this principle in the Final Act, to secure the consensus agreement that the accords required. The West then accepted the principle of "noninterference" in the internal affairs of other countries, as the ambiguous assurance to get Soviet agreement to the human rights provisions.

The diplomatic back-and-forth and the subtleties of language so many decades in the past can endure only as long as the signatories are willing to respect them. That ended on the day Russian forces launched their assault on the whole of Ukraine.

When the Soviet Union invaded Afghanistan at the end of 1979, the détente period of East-West accommodation was over. But Afghanistan was outside the European domain and in time, especially when the Soviet bloc weakened and imploded a decade or so later, cooperation and security standards in Europe again were considered the norm—until they no longer were.

That the Helsinki principles endured for nearly fifty years is itself remarkable. The Versailles peace treaty and the League of Nations not only were failures but also contributed to the onset of another world war only two decades later.

The Helsinki principles, as defined in M. E. Sarotte's examination of the circumstances around NATO expansion in *Not One Inch: America, Russia, and the Making of Post–Cold War Stalemate,* published (with extraordinary timeliness) as the Ukraine invasion started in 2022, were a factor in the intense negotiations over the reunification of Germany taking place in 1990.

Recalling the events around Soviet leader Mikhail Gorbachev's complaints about possible NATO expansion at a summit with President George H. W. Bush, Sarotte writes:

> Since Gorbachev was personally raising the subject of German, Central and Eastern European and Soviet membership in NATO, it would clearly be a contentious issue at the summit. Western leaders decided to use a riposte that [French president François] Mitterrand had already raised with Gorbachev: the so-called Helsinki Principle, the right guaranteed to all signatories of the Helsinki Final Act of 1975 to choose their own military alliances. During the Cold War, it had been a hollow promise, as Central and Eastern Europeans knew they were not free to choose anything but the Warsaw Pact. But on paper, at least, the Soviet Union had committed to this principle.

So as Basket Three had become the framework for human rights and other humanitarian issues, Basket One, on security, was a major factor in the years of Europe's realignment as the Soviet Union disappeared. And its abrogation returns Europe to the sort of conflicts that have marked its history for centuries.

Two institutions directly connected to the Helsinki Final Act were created in its aftermath. They are active and worthwhile but neither can be considered a major entity in the operations of the US or European governments.

The first was the Commission on Security and Cooperation in Europe—not to be confused by its initials with the conference that had inspired it—the unique entity that had members from both Congress and the State Department, a pairing of legislative and executive authority and interests. As described earlier, the origin of the commission was to hold the Soviet bloc accountable to the provisions of Basket Three on human rights, immigration, family reunification, and, broadly speaking, civil society.

The commission continues to operate, almost entirely now made up of members of Congress from both parties, with a staff of about fifteen, plus input from outside consultants and experts. Its annual budget of about $3 million is so small that its funding, not included in congressional funds because CSCE is considered an independent entity, has never been an issue. In fact, the strength of the commission, under the leadership since 2006 of staff director Kyle Parker, has been its ability to be influential on several policy issues without ever confronting the left-right splits that determine so much on Capitol Hill. The commission is bipartisan, with the commissioners chosen by the party leadership in the House and Senate. While a State Department representative is assigned to the commission, the executive branch no longer seems to fill its allotted slots as commissioners.

Parker says that the commission's greatest achievement in recent years was the Magnitsky Act of 2012, which sets out the terms of sanctions against, initially, Russians and later other global personalities found to be either abusers of human rights or financially corrupt. This story is told in a book by the financier Bill Browder, *Red Notice: A True Story of High Finance, Murder, and One Man's Fight for Justice*, published in 2015. Browder's Moscow-based lawyer, Sergei Magnitsky, was persecuted and eventually murdered in prison for his efforts to document the scale of Russian financial corruption.

Browder, with the commission's efforts, galvanized the instinctive suspicions about the interplay of power and corruption in Vladimir Putin's Russia to gain passage of the act. It was later adopted in thirty other countries and used against autocrats and oligarchs around the world. The commission was also a major factor in passage of the Trafficking Victims Protective Act in 2000 and legislation to counter anti-Semitism in Europe.

When the Magnitsky Act was passed, it was combined with the termination of the Jackson-Vanik legislation of the 1970s, which had set US-Soviet trade terms based on the number of Jews applying to leave the country who had received exit visas. That was thought no longer to be the factor that should determine Russia's "most-favored-nation" trade status.

Then, in 2022, all trade and other business contacts with Russia were upended by the invasion of Ukraine. When this era is now described as a new cold war, the designation is accurate, although it features an attempted military takeover and the renewal of threats of nuclear force.

Without the Helsinki Accords there would have been no Commission on Security and Cooperation in Europe or its contributions to the causes it supports. An examination of the historical record concludes that the organizational skill of the movement to support emigration of Soviet Jews to Israel and elsewhere made dissent in the Soviet era the public focus it became. And the Carter administration's specific attention to human rights, in the White House and at the State Department, was another element in moving these issues from the margins, where they had been in the past.

When the commission was established immediately after the Helsinki summit, its primary task was to track human rights compliance by the Soviet bloc. The activities of such great pillars of human rights like Andrei Sakharov or Václav Havel, already prominent in the 1970s, had started to attract broad support. Sakharov received the Nobel Peace Prize in 1975 but was not allowed to travel to accept the award. The forced exile of Alexandr Solzhenitsyn in 1973 also served as the momentum behind human rights and the Helsinki movements around the world. President Gerald Ford, as already described, had declined to meet Solzhenitsyn, but his successor, Jimmy Carter, wrote a letter to Sakharov in his early weeks as president and welcomed the former political prisoner Vladimir Bukovsky to the White House, a symbolic act that enraged the Kremlin.

That the full panoply of rights—civil, women's, LGBTQ, disability, Indigenous, economic, political, and others perhaps not yet identified—was recognized over time would suggest that the CSCE, conference and commission, were significant contributors to that process. Progress toward recognition of the rights of all people in all sorts of ways is one of the positive developments of the contemporary world.

The Organization for Security and Cooperation in Europe, the second of the two legacy institutions, was established in 1975 to further the goals of the Helsinki Accords. There are now fifty-seven member states from Europe, Eurasia, and North America. Its mission is to provide a "comprehensive approach to security, recognizing that peace and prosperity in the region depends on respect for the sovereignty and territorial integrity of the States as well as on respect for the human rights and fundamental freedoms of all individuals."

In 2022, the OSCE employed about 550 people in its Vienna headquarters and its associated Parliamentary Assembly and around 2,330 in its field operations monitoring events and trends in its region. Its most recent budget was roughly 138 million euros. It is part of the multilateral European infrastructure that also includes the European Union, NATO, the Organization for Economic Cooperation and Development, and the many Europe-based United Nations agencies and global enterprises like the World Health Organization, the World Trade Organization, and the International Labor Organization.

Taken together, these institutions are meant to monitor elections, a major focus, and to take steps to improve the security and conditions of life for the people living in Europe. That the OSCE exists so long after the Helsinki Accords were signed reflects the continuing efforts by civilization to govern itself and make headway against the profound conflicts that are the history of the world.

The war in Ukraine was central to the purview of the OSCE, and it immediately launched investigations into the conflict, with particular attention to International Humanitarian Law. On April 13, 2022, it released a 107-page preliminary report on violations of IHL and the evidence for

war crimes, with copious details of transgressions. Written
by three professors and based on the investigations by the
OSCE's field staff and observers, the report concluded that
IHL had been violated and war crimes committed. But its
findings were limited by the Russians' refusal to cooperate.
A letter to the professors and OSCE leadership from Alexander Lukashevich, the permanent Russian representative to
the OSCE, concludes by asserting that it is the Ukrainians
whose actions and statements "constitute direct advocacy and
war crimes."

International governmental bodies are only as meaningful as the willingness of its members to accept their mission.
That is why the role of an NGO with the scale and stature of
Human Rights Watch is the aspect of the Helsinki Accords
legacy that has proven to be most important.

That the commitment of a handful of Soviet citizens, their
counterparts in Eastern Europe, and a similarly small group
of Americans—private citizens and members of Congress and
the executive branch—could initiate so great a reality from a
document dismissed as insignificant is the tale worth the telling it has now received.

Coda

To RETURN TO our opening premise, the Helsinki Accords were just words in a document, agreed by the signatories but never ratified in the formal sense. Whatever our contemporary judgment about events as they happen, they should be revisited over time. That the Final Act has been instrumental to what is happening well into the twenty-first century is worthy of an account, an assessment, which the narrative has been, and we also contend, some celebration.

Appendix

Basket Three of the Helsinki Final Act

Co-operation in Humanitarian and Other Fields

The participating States,

Desiring to contribute to the strengthening of peace and understanding among peoples and to the spiritual enrichment of the human personality without distinction as to race, sex, language or religion,

Conscious that increased cultural and educational exchanges, broader dissemination of information, contacts between people, and the solution of humanitarian problems will contribute to the attainment of these aims,

Determined therefore to cooperate among themselves, irrespective of their political, economic and social systems, in order to create better conditions in the above fields, to develop and strengthen existing forms of co-operation and to work out new ways and means appropriate to these aims,

Convinced that this co-operation should take place in full respect for the principles guiding relations among participating States as set forth in the relevant document,

Have adopted the following:

1. Human Contacts   .

The participating States,

Considering the development of contacts to be an important element in the strengthening of friendly relations and trust among peoples,

Affirming, in relation to their present effort to improve conditions in this area, the importance they attach to humanitarian considerations,

Desiring in this spirit to develop, with the continuance of detente, further efforts to achieve continuing progress in this field,

And conscious that the questions relevant hereto must be settled by the States concerned under mutually acceptable conditions,

Make it their aim to facilitate freer movement and contacts, individually and collectively, whether privately or officially, among persons, institutions and organizations of the participating States, and to contribute to the solution of the humanitarian problems that arise in that connexion,

Declare their readiness to these ends to take measures which they consider appropriate and to conclude agreements or arrangements among themselves, as may be needed, and

Express their intention now to proceed to the implementation of the following:

(a) Contacts and Regular Meetings on the Basis of Family Ties

In order to promote further development of contacts on the basis of family ties the participating States will favourably consider applications for travel with the purpose of allowing persons to enter or leave their territory temporarily, and on a regular basis if desired, in order to visit members of their families.

Applications for temporary visits to meet members of their families will be dealt with without distinction as to the country of origin or destination: existing requirements for travel documents and visas will be applied in this spirit. The preparation and issue of such documents and visas will be effected within reasonable time limits, cases of urgent necessity—such as serious illness or death will be given priority treatment. They will take such steps as may be necessary to ensure that the fees for official travel documents and visas are acceptable.

They confirm that the presentation of an application concerning contacts on the basis of family ties will not modify the rights and obligations of the applicant or of members of his family.

(b) Reunification of Families

The participating States will deal in a positive and humanitarian spirit with the applications of persons who wish to be reunited with members of their family, with special attention being given to requests of an urgent character—such as requests submitted by persons who are ill or old.

They will deal with applications in this field as expeditiously as possible. They will lower where necessary the fees charged in connexion with these applications to ensure that they are at a moderate level.

Applications for the purpose of family reunification which are not granted may be renewed at the appropriate level and will be reconsidered at reasonably short intervals by the authorities of the country of residence or destination, whichever is concerned; under such circumstances fees will be charged only when applications are granted.

Persons whose applications for family reunification are granted may bring with them or ship their household and personal effects; to this end the participating States will use all possibilities provided by existing regulations.

Until members of the same family are reunited meetings and contacts between them may take place in accordance with the modalities for contacts on the basis of family ties.

The participating States will support the efforts of Red Cross and Red Crescent Societies concerned with the problems of family reunification.

They confirm that the presentation of an application concerning family reunification will not modify the rights and obligations of the applicant or of members of his family.

The receiving participating State will take appropriate care with regard to employment for persons from other participating States who take up permanent residence in that State in connexion with family reunification with its citizens and see that they are afforded opportunities equal to those enjoyed by its own citizens for education, medical assistance and social security.

(c) Marriage between Citizens of Different States

The participating States will examine favourably and on the basis of humanitarian considerations requests for exit or entry permits from persons who have decided to marry a citizen from another participating State.

The processing and issuing of the documents required for the above purposes and for the marriage will be in accordance with the provisions accepted for family reunification.

In dealing with requests from couples from different participating States, once married, to enable them and the minor children of their marriage to transfer their permanent residence to a State in which either one is normally a resident, the participating States will also apply the provisions accepted for family reunification.

(d) Travel for Personal or Professional Reasons

The participating States intend to facilitate wider travel by their citizens for personal or professional reasons and to this end they intend in particular:

- gradually to simplify and to administer flexibly the procedures for exit and entry;
- to ease regulations concerning movement of citizens from the other participating States in their territory, with due regard to security requirements.

They will endeavour gradually to lower, where necessary, the fees for visas and official travel documents.

They intend to consider, as necessary, means—including, in so far as appropriate, the conclusion of multilateral or bilateral consular conventions or other relevant agreements or understandings—for the improvement of arrangements to provide consular services, including legal and consular assistance.

* * *

They confirm that religious faiths, institutions and organizations, practising within the constitutional framework of the participating States, and their representatives can, in the field of their activities, have contacts and meetings among themselves and exchange information.

(e) Improvement of Conditions for Tourism
on an Individual or Collective Basis

The participating States consider that tourism contributes to a fuller knowledge of the life, culture and history of other countries, to the growth of understanding among peoples, to the improvement of contacts and to the broader use of leisure. They intend to promote the development of tourism, on an individual or collective basis, and, in particular, they intend:

- to promote visits to their respective countries by encouraging the provision of appropriate facilities and the simplification and expediting of necessary formalities relating to such visits;

- to increase, on the basis of appropriate agreements or arrangements where necessary, co-operation in the development of tourism, in particular by considering bilaterally possible ways to increase information relating to travel to other countries and to the reception and service of tourists, and other related questions of mutual interest.

(f) Meetings among Young People

The participating States intend to further the development of contacts and exchanges among young people by encouraging:

- increased exchanges and contacts on a short or long term basis among young people working, training or undergoing education through bilateral or multilateral agreements or regular programmes in all cases where it is possible;

- study by their youth organizations of the question of possible agreements relating to frameworks of multilateral youth co-operation;

- agreements or regular programmes relating to the organization of exchanges of students, of international youth seminars, of courses of professional training and foreign language study;

- the further development of youth tourism and the provision to this end of appropriate facilities;

- the development, where possible, of exchanges, contacts and co-operation on a bilateral or multilateral basis between their organizations which represent wide circles of young people working, training or undergoing education;

- awareness among youth of the importance of developing mutual understanding and of strengthening friendly relations and confidence among peoples.

(g) Sport

In order to expand existing links and co-operation in the field of sport the participating States will encourage contacts and exchanges of this kind, including sports meetings and competitions of all sorts, on the basis of the established international rules, regulations and practice.

(h) Expansion of Contacts

By way of further developing contacts among governmental institutions and non-governmental organizations and associations, including women's organizations, the participating States will facilitate the convening of meetings as well as travel by delegations, groups and individuals.

2. Information

The participating States,

Conscious of the need for an ever wider knowledge and understanding of the various aspects of life in other participating States,

Acknowledging the contribution of this process to the growth of confidence between peoples,

Desiring, with the development of mutual understanding between the participating States and with the further improvement of their relations, to continue further efforts towards progress in this field,

Recognizing the importance of the dissemination of information from the other participating States and of a better acquaintance with such information,

Emphasizing therefore the essential and influential role of the press, radio, television, cinema and news agencies and of the journalists working in these fields,

Make it their aim to facilitate the freer and wider dissemination of information of all kinds, to encourage co-operation in the field of information and the exchange of information with other countries, and to improve the conditions under which journalists from one participating State exercise their profession in another participating State, and

Express their intention in particular:

(a) Improvement of the Circulation of, Access to, and Exchange of Information

(i) Oral Information
To facilitate the dissemination of oral information through the encouragement of lectures and lecture tours by personalities and specialists from the other participating States, as well as exchanges of opinions at round table meetings, seminars, symposia, summer schools, congresses and other bilateral and multilateral meetings.

(ii) Printed Information

To facilitate the improvement of the dissemination, on their territory, of newspapers and printed publications, periodical and non-periodical, from the other participating States. For this purpose:

- they will encourage their competent firms and organizations to conclude agreements and contracts designed gradually to increase the quantities and the number of titles of newspapers and publications imported from the other participating States. These agreements and contracts should in particular mention the speediest conditions of delivery and the use of the normal channels existing in each country for the distribution of its own publications and newspapers, as well as forms and means of payment agreed between the parties making it possible to achieve the objectives aimed at by these agreements and contracts;

- where necessary, they will take appropriate measures to achieve the above objectives and to implement the provisions contained in the agreements and contracts.

To contribute to the improvement of access by the public to periodical and non periodical printed publications imported on the bases indicated above. In particular:

- they will encourage an increase in the number of places where these publications are on sale,

- they will facilitate the availability of these periodical publications during congresses, conferences, official visits and other international events and to tourists during the season;

- they will develop the possibilities for taking out subscriptions according to the modalities particular to each country;

- they will improve the opportunities for reading and borrowing these publications in large public libraries and their reading rooms as well as in university libraries.

They intend to improve the possibilities for acquaintance with bulletins of official information issued by diplomatic missions and distributed by those missions on the basis of arrangements acceptable to the interested parties.

(iii) Filmed and Broadcast Information
To promote the improvement of the dissemination of filmed and broadcast information. To this end:

- they will encourage the wider showing and broadcasting of a greater variety of recorded and filmed information from the other participating States, illustrating the various aspects of life in their countries and received on the basis of such agreements or arrangements as may be necessary between the organizations and firms directly concerned;

- they will facilitate the import by competent organizations and firms of recorded audio-visual material from the other participating States.

The participating States note the expansion in the dissemination of information broadcast by radio, and express the hope for the continuation of this process, so as to meet the interest of mutual understanding among peoples and the aims set forth by this Conference.

(b) Co-operation in the Field of Information

To encourage co-operation in the field of information on the basis of short or long term agreements or arrangements. In particular:

- they will favour increased co-operation among mass media organizations, including press agencies, as well as among publishing houses and organizations;

- they will favour co-operation among public or private, national or international radio and television organizations, in particular through the exchange of both live and recorded radio and television programmes, and through the joint production and the broadcasting and distribution of such programmes;

- they will encourage meetings and contacts both between journalists' organizations and between journalists from the participating States;

- they will view favourably the possibilities of arrangements between periodical publications as well as between newspapers from the participating States, for the purpose of exchanging and publishing articles;

- they will encourage the exchange of technical information as well as the organization of joint research and meetings devoted to the exchange of experience and views between experts in the field of the press, radio and television.

(c) Improvement of Working Conditions for Journalists

The participating States, desiring to improve the conditions under which journalists from one participating State exercise their profession in another participating State, intend in particular to:

- examine in a favourable spirit and within a suitable and reasonable time scale requests from journalists for visas;

- grant to permanently accredited journalists of the participating States, on the basis of arrangements, multiple entry and exit visas for specified periods;

- facilitate the issue to accredited journalists of the participating States of permits for stay in their country of temporary residence and, if and when these are necessary, of other official papers which it is appropriate for them to have;

- ease, on a basis of reciprocity, procedures for arranging travel by journalists of the participating States in the country where they are exercising their profession, and to provide progressively greater opportunities for such travel, subject to the observance of regulations relating to the existence of areas closed for security reasons;

- ensure that requests by such journalists for such travel receive, in so far as possible, an expeditious response, taking into account the time scale of the request;

- increase the opportunities for journalists of the participating States to communicate personally with their sources, including organizations and official institutions;

- grant to journalists of the participating States the right to import, subject only to its being taken out again, the technical equipment (photographic, cinematographic, tape recorder, radio and television) necessary for the exercise of their profession;*

- enable journalists of the other participating States, whether permanently or temporarily accredited, to transmit completely, normally and rapidly by means recognized by the participating States to the information organs which they represent, the results of their professional activity, including tape recordings and undeveloped film, for the purpose of publication or of broadcasting on the radio or television.

The participating States reaffirm that the legitimate pursuit of their professional activity will neither render journalists liable to expulsion nor otherwise penalize them. If an accredited journalist is expelled, he will be informed of the reasons for this act and may submit an application for re-examination of his case.

---

*While recognizing that appropriate local personnel are employed by foreign journalists in many instances, the participating States note that the above provisions would be applied, subject to the observance of the appropriate rules, to persons from the other participating States, who are regularly and professionally engaged as technicians, photographers or cameramen of the press, radio, television or cinema.

3. Co-operation and Exchanges
in the Field of Culture

The participating States

Considering that cultural exchanges and co-operation contribute to a better comprehension among people and among peoples, and thus promote a lasting understanding among States,

Confirming the conclusions already formulated in this field at the multilateral level, particularly at the Intergovernmental Conference on Cultural Policies in Europe, organized by UNESCO in Helsinki in June 1972, where interest was manifested in the active participation of the broadest possible social groups in an increasingly diversified cultural life,

Desiring, with the development of mutual confidence and the further improvement of relations between the participating States, to continue further efforts toward progress in this field,

Disposed in this spirit to increase substantially their cultural exchanges, with regard both to persons and to cultural works, and to develop among them an active co-operation, both at the bilateral and the multilateral level, in all the fields of culture,

Convinced that such a development of their mutual relations will contribute to the enrichment of the respective cultures, while respecting the originality of each, as well as to the reinforcement among them of a consciousness of common values, while continuing to develop cultural co-operation with other countries of the world,

Declare that they jointly set themselves the following objectives:

(a) to develop the mutual exchange of information with a view to a better knowledge of respective cultural achievements,

(b) to improve the facilities for the exchange and for the dissemination of cultural property,

(c) to promote access by all to respective cultural achievements,

(d) to develop contacts and co-operation among persons active in the field of culture,

(e) to seek new fields and forms of cultural co-operation,

Thus *give expression to* their common will to take progressive, coherent and longterm action in order to achieve the objectives of the present declaration; and

Express their intention now to proceed to the implementation of the following:

Extension of Relations

To expand and improve at the various levels co-operation and links in the field of culture, in particular by:

• concluding, where appropriate, agreements on a bilateral or multilateral basis, providing for the extension of relations among competent State institutions and non-governmental organizations in the field of culture, as well as among people engaged in cultural activities, taking into account the need both for flexibility and the fullest possible use of existing agreements, and bearing in mind that agreements and also other arrangements constitute important means of developing cultural cooperation and exchanges;

- contributing to the development of direct communication and co-operation among relevant State institutions and non-governmental organizations, including, where necessary, such communication and co-operation carried out on the basis of special agreements and arrangements;

- encouraging direct contacts and communications among persons engaged in cultural activities, including, where necessary, such contacts and communications carried out on the basis of special agreements, and arrangements.

Mutual Knowledge

Within their competence to adopt, on a bilateral and multilateral level, appropriate measures which would give their peoples a more comprehensive and complete mutual knowledge of their achievements in the various fields of culture, and among them:

- to examine jointly, if necessary with the assistance of appropriate international organizations, the possible creation in Europe and the structure of a bank of cultural data, which would collect information from the participating countries and make it available to its correspondents on their request, and to convene for this purpose a meeting of experts from interested States;

- to consider, if necessary in conjunction with appropriate international organizations, ways of compiling in Europe

an inventory of documentary films of a cultural or
scientific nature from the participating States;

- to encourage more frequent book exhibitions and to
  examine the possibility of organizing periodically in
  Europe a large-scale exhibition of books from the
  participating States;

- to promote the systematic exchange, between the
  institutions concerned and publishing houses, of
  catalogues of available books as well as of pre-publication
  material which will include, as far as possible, all
  forthcoming publications; and also to promote the
  exchange of material between firms publishing
  encyclopaedias, with a view to improving the presentation
  of each country;

- to examine jointly questions of expanding and improving
  exchanges of information in the various fields of culture,
  such as theatre, music, library work as well as the
  conservation and restoration of cultural property.

Exchanges and Dissemination

To contribute to the improvement of facilities for exchanges
and the dissemination of cultural property, by appropriate
means, in particular by:

- studying the possibilities for harmonizing and reducing
  the charges relating to international commercial
  exchanges of books and other cultural materials, and
  also for new means of insuring works of art in foreign

exhibitions and for reducing the risks of damage or loss to which these works are exposed by their movement;

- facilitating the formalities of customs clearance, in good time for programmes of artistic events, of the works of art, materials and accessories appearing on lists agreed upon by the organizers of these events;

- encouraging meetings among representatives of competent organizations and relevant firms to examine measures within their field of activity—such as the simplification of orders, time limits for sending supplies and modalities of payment—which might facilitate international commercial exchanges of books;

- promoting the loan and exchange of films among their film institutes and film libraries;

- encouraging the exchange of information among interested parties concerning events of a cultural character foreseen in the participating States, in fields where this is most appropriate, such as music, theatre and the plastic and graphic arts, with a view to contributing to the compilation and publication of a calendar of such events, with the assistance, where necessary, of the appropriate international organizations;

- encouraging a study of the impact which the foreseeable development, and a possible harmonization among interested parties, of the technical means used for the dissemination of culture might have on the development of cultural co-operation and exchanges, while keeping in view the preservation of the diversity and originality, of their respective cultures;

- encouraging, in the way they deem appropriate, within their cultural policies, the further development of interest in the cultural heritage of the other participating States, conscious of the merits and the value of each culture;

- endeavouring to ensure the full and effective application of the international agreements and conventions on copyrights and on circulation of cultural property to which they are party or to which they may decide in the future to become party.

Access

To promote fuller mutual access by all to the achievements— works, experiences and performing arts—in the various fields of culture of their countries, and to that end to make the best possible efforts, in accordance with their competence, more particularly:

- to promote wider dissemination of books and artistic works, in particular by such means as:

  - facilitating, while taking full account of the international copyright conventions to which they are party, international contacts and communications between authors and publishing houses as well as other cultural institutions, with a view to a more complete mutual access to cultural achievements;

  - recommending that, in determining the size of editions, publishing houses take into account also the demand from the other participating States, and that rights of sale in other participating States be granted, where possible, to several sales organizations of the importing countries, by agreement between interested partners;

- encouraging competent organizations and relevant firms to conclude agreements and contracts and contributing, by this means, to a gradual increase in the number and diversity of works by authors from the other participating States available in the original and in translation in their libraries and bookshops;

- promoting, where deemed appropriate, an increase in the number of sales outlets where books by authors from the other participating States, imported in the original on the basis of agreements and contracts, and in translation, are for sale;

- promoting, on a wider scale, the translation of works in the sphere of literature and other fields of cultural activity, produced in the languages of the other participating States, especially from the less widely-spoken languages, and the publication and dissemination of the translated works by such measures as:

  - encouraging more regular contacts between interested publishing houses; developing their efforts in the basic and advanced training of translators;

  - encouraging, by appropriate means, the publishing houses of their countries to publish translations;

  - facilitating the exchange between publishers and interested institutions of lists of books which might be translated;

- promoting between their countries the professional activity and co-operation of translators;

- carrying out joint studies on ways of further promoting translations and their dissemination;

- improving and expanding exchanges of books, bibliographies and catalogue cards between libraries;

• to envisage other appropriate measures which would permit, where necessary by mutual agreement among interested parties, the facilitation of access to their respective cultural achievements, in particular in the field of books;

• to contribute by appropriate means to the wider use of the mass media in order to improve mutual acquaintance with the cultural life of each;

• to seek to develop the necessary conditions for migrant workers and their families to preserve their links with their national culture, and also to adapt themselves to their new cultural environment;

• to encourage the competent bodies and enterprises to make a wider choice and effect wider distribution of full-length and documentary films from the other participating States, and to promote more frequent non-commercial showings, such as premieres, film weeks and festivals, giving due consideration to films from countries whose cinematographic works are less well known;

• to promote, by appropriate means, the extension of opportunities for specialists from the other participating States to work with materials of a cultural character from film and audio-visual archives, within the framework of the existing rules for work on such archival materials;

- to encourage a joint study by interested bodies, where appropriate with the assistance of the competent international organizations, of the expediency and the conditions for the establishment of a repertory of their recorded television programmes of a cultural nature, as well as of the means of viewing them rapidly in order to facilitate their selection and possible acquisition.

Contacts and Co-operation

To contribute, by appropriate means, to the development of contacts and co-operation in the various fields of culture, especially among creative artists and people engaged in cultural activities, in particular by making efforts to:

- promote for persons active in the field of culture, travel and meetings including, where necessary, those carried out on the basis of agreements, contracts or other special arrangements and which are relevant to their cultural co-operation;

- encourage in this way contacts among creative and performing artists and artistic groups with a view to their working together, making known their works in other participating States or exchanging views on topics relevant to their common activity;

- encourage, where necessary through appropriate arrangements, exchanges of trainee and specialists and the granting of scholarships for basic and advanced

training in various fields of culture such as the arts and
architecture, museums and libraries, literary studies and
translation, and contribute to the creation of favourable
conditions of reception in their respective institutions;

- encourage the exchange of experience in the training of
  organizers of cultural activities as well as of teachers and
  specialists in fields such as theatre, opera, ballet, music
  and fine arts;

- continue to encourage the organization of international
  meetings among creative artists, especially young creative
  artists, on current questions of artistic and literary
  creation which are of interest for joint study;

- study other possibilities for developing exchanges and
  co-operation among persons active in the field of culture,
  with a view to a better mutual knowledge of the cultural
  life of the participating States.

Fields and Forms of Co-operation

To encourage the search for new fields and forms of cultural
co-operation, to these ends contributing to the conclusion
among interested parties, where necessary, of appropriate
agreements and arrangements, and in this context to promote:

- joint studies regarding cultural policies, in particular in
  their social aspects, and as they relate to planning, town-
  planning, educational and environmental policies, and
  the cultural aspects of tourism;

- the exchange of knowledge in the realm of cultural diversity, with a view to contributing thus to a better understanding by interested parties of such diversity where it occurs;

- the exchange of information, and as may be appropriate, meetings of experts, the elaboration and the execution of research programmes and projects, as well as their joint evaluation, and the dissemination of the results, on the subjects indicated above;

  - such forms of cultural co-operation and the development of such joint projects as: international events in the fields of the plastic and graphic arts, cinema, theatre, ballet, music, folklore, etc.; book fairs and exhibitions, joint performances of operatic and dramatic works, as well as performances given by soloists, instrumental ensembles, orchestras, choirs and other artistic groups, including those composed of amateurs, paying due attention to the organization of international cultural youth events and the exchange of young artists;

  - the inclusion of works by writers and composers from the other participating States in the repertoires of soloists and artistic ensembles;

  - the preparation, translation and publication of articles, studies and monographs, as well as of low-cost books and of artistic and literary collections, suited to making better known respective cultural achievements, envisaging for this purpose meetings among experts and representatives of publishing houses;

- the co-production and the exchange of films and of radio and television programmes, by promoting, in particular, meetings among producers, technicians and representatives of the public authorities with a view to working out favourable conditions for the execution of specific joint projects and by encouraging, in the field of co-production, the establishment of international filming teams;

- the organization of competitions for architects and town-planners, bearing in mind the possible implementation of the best projects and the formation, where possible, of international teams;

- the implementation of joint projects for conserving, restoring and showing to advantage works of art, historical and archaeological monuments and sites of cultural interest, with the help, in appropriate cases, of international organizations of a governmental or non-governmental character as well as of private institutions—competent and active in these fields— envisaging for this purpose:

  · periodic meetings of experts of the interested parties to elaborate the necessary proposals, while bearing in mind the need to consider these questions in a wider social and economic context;

  · the publication in appropriate periodicals of articles designed to make known and to compare, among the participating States, the most significant achievements and innovations;

  · a joint study with a view to the improvement and possible harmonization of the different systems used to inventory and catalogue the historical monuments and places of cultural interest in their countries;

· the study of the possibilities for organizing international courses for the training of specialists in different disciplines relating to restoration.

* * *

National minorities or regional cultures. The participating States, recognizing the contribution that national minorities or regional cultures can make to co-operation among them in various fields of culture, intend, when such minorities or cultures exist within their territory, to facilitate this contribution, taking into account the legitimate interests of their members.

4. Co-operation and Exchanges in the Field of Education

The participating States,

Conscious that the development of relations of an international character in the fields of education and science contributes to a better mutual understanding and is to the advantage of all peoples as well as to the benefit of future generations,

Prepared to facilitate, between organizations, institutions and persons engaged in education and science, the further development of exchanges of knowledge and experience as well as of contacts, on the basis of special arrangements where these are necessary,

Desiring to strengthen the links among educational and scientific establishments and also to encourage their co-operation in sectors of common interest, particularly where the levels of knowledge and resources require efforts to be concerted internationally, and

Convinced that progress in these fields should be accompanied and supported by a wider knowledge of foreign languages,

Express to these ends their intention in particular:

(a) Extension of Relations

To expand and improve at the various levels co-operation and links in the fields of education and science, in particular by:

- concluding, where appropriate, bilateral or multilateral agreements providing for co-operation and exchanges among State institutions, non-governmental bodies and persons engaged in activities in education and science, bearing in mind the need both for flexibility and the fuller use of existing agreements and arrangements;

- promoting the conclusion of direct arrangements between universities and other institutions of higher education and research, in the framework of agreements between governments where appropriate;

- encouraging among persons engaged in education and science direct contacts and communications including those based on special agreements or arrangements where these are appropriate.

(b) Access and Exchanges

To improve access, under mutually acceptable conditions, for students, teachers and scholars of the participating States to each other's educational, cultural and scientific institutions, and to intensify exchanges among these institutions in all areas of common interest, in particular by:

- increasing the exchange of information on facilities for study and courses open to foreign participants, as well as on the conditions under which they will be admitted and received;

- facilitating travel between the participating States by scholars, teachers and students for purposes of study, teaching and research as well as for improving knowledge of each other's educational, cultural and scientific achievements;

- encouraging the award of scholarships for study, teaching and research in their countries to scholars, teachers and students of other participating States;

- establishing, developing or encouraging programmes providing for the broader exchange of scholars, teachers and students, including the organization of symposia, seminars and collaborative projects, and the exchanges of educational and scholarly information such as university publications and materials from libraries;

- promoting the efficient implementation of such arrangements and programmes by providing scholars, teachers and students in good time with more detailed information about their placing in universities and institutes and the programmes envisaged for them; by granting them the opportunity to use relevant scholarly, scientific and open archival materials; and by facilitating their travel within the receiving State for the purpose of study or research as well as in the form of vacation tours on the basis of the usual procedures;

- promoting a more exact assessment of the problems of comparison and equivalence of academic degrees and diplomas by fostering the exchange of information on the organization, duration and content of studies, the comparison of methods of assessing levels of knowledge, and academic qualifications, and, where feasible, arriving at the mutual recognition of academic degrees and diplomas either through governmental agreements, where necessary, or direct arrangements between universities and other institutions of higher learning and research;

- recommending, moreover, to the appropriate international organizations that they should intensify their efforts to reach a generally acceptable solution to the problems of comparison and equivalence between academic degrees and diplomas.

(c) Science

Within their competence to broaden and improve co-operation and exchanges in the field of science, in particular:

To increase, on a bilateral or multilateral basis, the exchange and dissemination of scientific information and documentation by such means as:

- making this information more widely available to scientists and research workers of the other participating States through, for instance, participation in international information sharing programmes or through other appropriate arrangements;

- broadening and facilitating the exchange of samples and other scientific materials used particularly for fundamental research in the fields of natural sciences and medicine;

- inviting scientific institutions and universities to keep each other more fully and regularly informed about their current and contemplated research work in fields of common interest.

To facilitate the extension of communications and direct contacts between universities, scientific institutions and associations as well as among scientists and research workers, including those based where necessary on special agreements or arrangements, by such means as:

- further developing exchanges of scientists and research workers and encouraging the organization of preparatory meetings or working groups on research topics of common interest;

- encouraging the creation of joint teams of scientists to pursue research projects under arrangements made by the scientific institutions of several countries;

- assisting the organization and successful functioning of international conferences and seminars and participation in them by their scientists and research workers;

- furthermore envisaging, in the near future, a "Scientific Forum" in the form of a meeting of leading personalities in science from the participating States to discuss interrelated problems of common interest concerning current and future developments in science, and to promote the expansion of contacts, communications and the exchange of information between scientific institutions and among scientists;

- foreseeing, at an early date, a meeting of experts representing the participating States and their national scientific institutions, in order to prepare such a "Scientific Forum" in consultation with appropriate international organizations, such as UNESCO and the ECE;

- considering in due course what further steps might be taken with respect to the "Scientific Forum."

To develop in the field of scientific research, on a bilateral or multilateral basis, the co-ordination of programmes carried out in the participating States and the organization of joint programmes, especially in the areas mentioned below, which may involve the combined efforts of scientists and in certain cases the use of costly or unique equipment. The list of subjects in these areas is illustrative; and specific projects would have to be determined subsequently by the potential partners in the participating States, taking account of the contribution which could be made by appropriate international organizations and scientific institutions:

- *exact and natural sciences,* in particular fundamental research in such fields as mathematics, physics, theoretical physics, geophysics, chemistry, biology, ecology and astronomy;

- *medicine,* in particular basic research into cancer and cardiovascular diseases, studies on the diseases endemic in the developing countries, as well as medico-social research with special emphasis on occupational diseases, the rehabilitation of the handicapped and the care of mothers, children and the elderly;

- *the humanities and social sciences,* such as history, geography, philosophy, psychology, pedagogical research, linguistics, sociology, the legal, political and economic sciences; comparative studies on social, socioeconomic and cultural phenomena which are of common interest to the participating States, especially the problems of human environment and urban development; and scientific studies on the methods of conserving and restoring monuments and works of art.

(d) Foreign Languages and Civilizations

To encourage the study of foreign languages and civilizations as an important means of expanding communication among peoples for their better acquaintance with the culture of each country, as well as for the strengthening of international co-operation; to this end to stimulate, within their competence, the further development and improvement of foreign language teaching and the diversification of choice of languages taught at various levels, paying due attention to less widely-spread or studied languages, and in particular:

- to intensify co-operation aimed at improving the teaching of foreign languages through exchanges of information and experience concerning the development and application of effective modem teaching methods and technical aids, adapted to the needs of different categories of students, including methods of accelerated teaching; and to consider the possibility of conducting, on a bilateral or multilateral basis, studies of new methods of foreign language teaching;

- to encourage co-operation between institutions concerned, on a bilateral or multilateral basis, aimed at exploiting more fully the resources of modem educational technology in language teaching, for example through comparative studies by their specialists and, where agreed, through exchanges or transfers of audio-visual materials, of materials used for preparing textbooks, as well as of information about new types of technical equipment used for teaching languages;

- to promote the exchange of information on the experience acquired in the training of language teachers and to intensify exchanges on a bilateral basis of language teachers and students as well as to facilitate their participation in summer courses in languages and civilizations, wherever these are organized;

- to encourage co-operation among experts in the field of lexicography with the aim of defining the necessary terminological equivalents, particularly in the scientific and technical disciplines, in order to facilitate relations among scientific institutions and specialists;

- to promote the wider spread of foreign language study among the different types of secondary education establishments and greater possibilities of choice between an increased number of European languages; and in this context to consider, wherever appropriate, the possibilities for developing the recruitment and training of teachers as well as the organization of the student groups required;

- to favour, in higher education, a wider choice in the languages offered to language students and greater opportunities for other students to study various foreign languages; also to facilitate, where desirable, the organization of courses in languages and civilizations, on the basis of special arrangements as necessary to be given by foreign lecturers, particularly from European countries having less widely-spread or studied languages;

- to promote, within the framework of adult education, the further development of specialized programmes, adapted to various needs and interests, for teaching foreign languages to their own inhabitants and the languages of host countries to interested adults from other countries; in this context to encourage interested institutions to cooperate, for example, in the elaboration of programmes for teaching by radio and television and by accelerated methods, and also, where desirable, in the definition of study objectives for such programmes, with a view to arriving at comparable levels of language proficiency;

- to encourage the association, where appropriate, of the teaching of foreign languages with the study of the corresponding civilizations and also to make further efforts to stimulate interest in the study of foreign languages, including relevant out-of-class activities.

(e) Teaching Methods

To promote the exchange of experience, on a bilateral or multilateral basis, in teaching methods at all levels of education, including those used in permanent and adult education, as well as the exchange of teaching materials, in particular by:

- further developing various forms of contacts and co-operation in the different fields of pedagogical science, for example through comparative or joint studies carried out by interested institutions or through exchanges of information on the results of teaching experiments;

- intensifying exchanges of information on teaching methods used in various educational systems and on results of research into the processes by which pupils and students acquire knowledge, taking account of relevant experience in different types of specialized education;

- facilitating exchanges of experience concerning the organization and functioning of education intended for adults and recurrent education, the relationships between these and other forms and levels of education, as well as concerning the means of adapting education, including vocational and technical training, to the needs of economic and social development in their countries;

- adults in international understanding, with particular reference to those major problems of mankind whose solution calls for a common approach and wider international co-operation;

- encouraging exchanges of teaching materials—including school textbooks, having in mind the possibility of promoting mutual knowledge and facilitating the presentation of each country in such books—as well as exchanges of information on technical innovations in the field of education.

* * *

National minorities or regional cultures. The participating States, recognizing the contribution that national minorities or regional cultures can make to co-operation among them in various fields of education, intend, when such minorities or cultures exist within their territory, to facilitate this contribution, taking into account the legitimate interests of their members.

Selected Bibliography

Books

Arbatov, Georgi. *The System: An Insider's Life in Soviet Politics.*
Introduction by Strobe Talbott. New York: Times Books/
Random House, 1992.

Banac, Ivo, ed. *Eastern Europe in Revolution.* Ithaca, NY: Cornell
University Press, 1992.

Beamish, Tufton, and Guy Hadley. *The Kremlin's Dilemma: The
Struggle for Human Rights in Eastern Europe.* San Rafael, CA:
Presidio Press, 1979.

Beckerman, Gal. *The Quiet Before: On the Unexpected Origins of
Radical Ideas.* New York: Crown, 2022.

Behr, Edward. *Kiss the Hand You Cannot Bite: The Rise and Fall of the
Ceaușescus.* New York: Villard Books, 1991.

Belton, Catherine. *Putin's People: How the KGB Took Back Russia and
Then Took on the West.* London: William Collins, 2020.

Bernhard, Michael H. *The Origins of Democratization in Poland:
Workers, Intellectuals, and Oppositional Politics, 1976–1980.* New
York: Columbia University Press, 1993.

Bernstein, Robert L., with Doug Merlino. *Speaking Freely: My Life
in Publishing and Human Rights.* Foreword by Toni Morrison.
New York: New Press, 2016.

Bohley, Bärbel, et al. *40 Jahre DDR und die Bürger melden sich zu
Wort.* Frankfurt am Main: Büchergilde Gutenberg, 1989.

Browder, Bill. *Red Notice: A True Story of High Finance, Murder, and
One Man's Fight for Justice.* New York: Simon & Schuster, 2015.

Curry, Jane Leftwich, ed. *Dissent in Eastern Europe.* New York:
Praeger, 1983.

DDR: Das Manifest der Opposition: Eine Dokumentation. Munich: Wilhelm Goldmann Verlag, 1978.

Deletant, Dennis. *Ceaușescu and the Securitate: Coercion and Dissent in Romania, 1965–1989.* New York: M.E. Sharpe, 1995.

Dobrynin, Anatoly. *In Confidence: Moscow's Ambassador to Six Cold War Presidents.* New York: Times Books/Random House, 1995.

Doder, Dusko. *Shadows and Whispers: Power Politics Inside the Kremlin from Brezhnev to Gorbachev.* New York: Random House, 1986.

Ehring, Klaus, and Martin Dallwitz. *Scherter zu Pflugscharen: Friedensbewegung in der DDR.* Reinbek bein Hamburg: Rowohlt, 1982.

Fainberg, Dina. *Cold War Correspondents: Soviet and American Reporters on the Ideological Frontlines.* Baltimore: Johns Hopkins University Press, 2020.

Fehér, Ferenc, and Andrew Arato, eds. *Crisis and Reform in Eastern Europe.* New Brunswick, NJ: Transaction, 1991.

Fisher, Mary Ellen. *Nicolae Ceaușescu: A Study in Political Leadership.* Boulder, CO: L. Rienner, 1989.

Fulbrook, Mary. *Anatomy of a Dictatorship: Inside the GDR 1949–1989.* Oxford: Oxford University Press, 1995.

Garton Ash, Timothy. *The Magic Lantern: The Revolution of '89 Witnessed in Warsaw, Budapest, Berlin, and Prague.* New York: Vintage Books, 1993.

———. *The Polish Revolution: Solidarity.* New York: Vintage Books, 1983.

———. *The Uses of Adversity: Essays on the Fate of Central Europe.* New York: Random House, 1989.

Georgescu, Vlad. *Istoria Românilor de la Origini Pînă în Zilele Noastre.* American-Romanian Academy of Arts and Sciences, Vol. 4, 1984.

———. *Romania: 40 Years (1944–84).* New York: Praeger, 1985.

Goeckel, Robert F. *The Lutheran Church and the East German State: Political Conflict and Change under Ulbricht and Honecker.* Ithaca, NY: Cornell University Press, 1991.

Goma, Paul. *Le Tremblement des Hommes: peut-on vivre en Roumanie aujourd'hui?* Paris: Éditions du Seuil, 1979.

Grachev, Andrei. *Gorbachev's Gamble: Soviet Foreign Policy and the End of the Cold War*. Malden, MA: Polity Press, 2008.

Hajek, Jiri. *Dix ans après: Prague 1968–1978*. Paris: Editions du Seuil, 1978.

Harrington, Joseph F., and Bruce J. Courtney. *Tweaking the Nose of the Russians: Fifty Years of American-Romanian Relations, 1940–1990*. New York: Columbia University Press, 1991.

Havel, Václav. *Disturbing the Peace: A Conversation with Karel Hvizdala*. New York: Alfred A. Knopf, 1990.

———, et al. *The Power of the Powerless: Citizens against the State in Central-Eastern Europe*. New York: Routledge, 2015.

Hoffman, David E. *The Oligarchs: Wealth and Power in the New Russia*. New York: PublicAffairs, 2002.

King, Robert R., and James F. Brown, eds. *Eastern Europe's Uncertain Future: A Selection of Radio Free Europe Research Reports*. New York: Praeger, 1977.

Kopelev, Lev. *To Be Preserved Forever*. Foreword by Lillian Hellman. Afterword by Robert G. Kaiser. Philadelphia and New York: J. B. Lippincott, 1977.

Korey, William. *The Promises We Keep: Human Rights, The Helsinki Process, and American Foreign Policy*. New York: St. Martin's Press, 1993.

Kusin, Vladimir V. *From Dubcek to Charter 77: A Study of "Normalization" in Czechoslovakia*. New York: St. Martin's Press, 1978.

Laber, Jeri. *The Courage of Strangers: Coming of Age with the Human Rights Movement*. Foreword by Václav Havel. New York: PublicAffairs, 2002.

Levesque, Jacques. *The Enigma of 1989: The USSR and the Liberation of Eastern Europe*. Berkeley: University of California Press, 1997.

Lipski, Jan Jozef. *KOR: A History of the Workers' Defense Committee in Poland, 1976–1981*. Berkeley: University of California Press, 1985.

Maresca, John J. *To Helsinki: The Conference on Security and Cooperation in Europe, 1973–1975*. Foreword by William E. Griffith. Durham. NC: Duke University Press, 1985.

———. *Helsinki Revisited: A Key U.S. Negotiator's Memoirs on the Development of the CSCE into the OSCE*. Stuttgart: Ibidem-Verlag, 2016.

McDermott, Kevin, and Matthew Stibbe. *Revolution and Resistance in Eastern Europe: Challenges to Communist Rule.* New York: Berg, 2006.

Michnik, Adam. "The Moral and Spiritual Origins of Solidarity." In *Without Force or Lies: Voices from the Revolution of Central Europe in 1989–90.* Edited by William M. Brinton and Alan Rinzler. San Francisco: Mercury House, 1990.

Morgan, Michael Cotey. *The Final Act: The Helsinki Accords and the Transformation of the Cold War.* Princeton: Princeton University Press, 2018.

Neier, Aryeh. *The International Human Rights Movement: A History.* Princeton: Princeton University Press, 2020.

———. *Taking Liberties: Four Decades in the Struggle for Rights.* New York: PublicAffairs, 2003.

Opp, Karl-Dieter, Peter Voss, and Christiane Gern. *Origins of a Spontaneous Revolution: East Germany, 1989.* Ann Arbor, MI: University of Michigan Press, 1995.

Osnos, Peter L. W. *An Especially Good View: Watching History Happen.* New York: Platform, 2021.

Philipsen, Dirk. *We Were the People: Voices from East Germany's Revolutionary Autumn of 1989.* Durham, NC: Duke University Press, 1993.

Putin, Vladimir. *First Person: An Astonishingly Frank Self-Portrait by Russia's President.* Translated by Catherine Fitzpatrick. New York: PublicAffairs, 2000.

Raina, Peter. *Independent Social Movements in Poland.* London: London School of Economics and Political Science, 1981.

———. *Political Opposition in Poland, 1954–1977.* London: Poets and Painters Press, 1978.

Sakharov, Andrei. *Memoirs.* New York: Alfred A. Knopf, 1990.

Sarotte, M. E. *Not One Inch: America, Russia, and the Making of Post-Cold War Stalemate.* New Haven, CT: Yale University Press, 2021.

Schlotter, Peter. *Die KSZE im Ost-West Konflikt: Wirkung einer internationalen Institution.* Franfurt am Main: Campus, 1999.

Sharansky, Natan. *Fear No Evil.* New York: Random House, 1988.

————, with Ron Dermer. *The Case for Democracy: The Power of Freedom to Overcome Tyranny and Terror.* New York: PublicAffairs, 2004.

————, and Gil Troy. *Never Alone: Prison, Politics, and My People.* New York: PublicAffairs, 2020.

Sherer, Carroll Russell. *A Great Adventure: Thirty Years in Diplomatic Service.* Greenwich, CT, 2007.

Skilling, H. Gordon. *Charter 77 and Human Rights in Czechoslovakia.* London: Allen & Unwin, 1981.

Snyder, Sarah B. *Human Rights Activism and the End of the Cold War: A Transnational History of the Helsinki Network.* Cambridge: Cambridge University Press, 2011.

Stokes, Gale. *The Walls Came Tumbling Down.* New York: Oxford University Press, 1993.

Thomas, Daniel C. *The Helsinki Effect: International Norms, Human Rights, and the Demise of Communism.* Princeton: Princeton University Press, 2001.

Tismăneanu, Vladimir. *Reinventing Politics: Eastern Europe from Stalin to Havel.* New York: Free Press, 1992.

————. *Stalinism for All Seasons: A Political History of Romanian Communism.* Berkeley: University of California Press, 2003.

Tokes, Rudolf L., ed. *Opposition in Eastern Europe.* Baltimore: Johns Hopkins University Press, 1979.

Torpey, John C. *Intellectuals, Socialism, and Dissent: The East German Opposition and Its Legacy.* Minneapolis: University of Minnesota Press, 1995.

Wenger, Andreas, Vojtech Mastny, and Christian Nuenlist, eds. *Origins of the European Security System: The Helsinki Process Revisited, 1965–75.* New York: Routledge, 2008.

Yeltsin, Boris. *Midnight Diaries.* Translated by Catherine Fitzpatrick. New York: PublicAffairs, 2000.

————. *The Struggle for Russia.* New York: Times Books/Random House, 1994.

Zuzowski, Robert. *Political Dissent and Opposition in Poland: The Workers' Defense Committee "KOR."* Westport, CT: Praeger, 1992.

Articles

Amalrik, Andrei. "News from Moscow." *New York Review of Books*, March 25, 1971.

Birnbaum, Karl E. "Human Rights and East-West Relations." *Foreign Affairs* 55, no. 4 (July 1977): 783–99.

Bogert, Carroll. "Human Rights Advocacy in Global Governance: A Case Study of Human Rights Watch." In James P. Muldoon Jr. et al., eds. *The New Dynamics of Multilateralism: Diplomacy, International Organizations, and Global Governance.* New York: Routledge, 2011.

Browne, Malcolm W. "Belgrade Parley: Few Hopes," *New York Times*, August 6, 1977.

Cole, Wade M. "No News Is Good News: Human Rights Coverage in the American Print Media, 1980–2000." *Journal of Human Rights*, 2010.

"Conscience contre existence: Information à propos de la naissance et de l'évolution de la Charte 77." *Cahiers de l'Est* 9/10 (1977).

"Diplomacy: A Star-Studded Summit Spectacular." *Time*, August 4, 1975.

Dixon, Robyn. "Leading Russian Dissident and Putin Critic Sergei Kovalyov Dies at 91." *Washington Post*, August 11, 2021.

Fascell, Dante B. "Did Human Rights Survive Belgrade?" *Foreign Policy* 31 (Summer 1978): 104–18.

Galey, Margaret E. "Congress, Foreign Policy and Human Rights Ten Years after Helsinki." *Human Rights Quarterly* 7, no. 3 (August 1985): 334–72.

"Helsinki Accord's Echo in Eastern Europe." *Financial Times*, January 12, 1977.

Hirschman, Albert O. "Exit, Voice and the Fate of the German Democratic Republic," *World Politics* 45, no. 2 (January 1993): 173–202.

Klenner, Hermann. "Menschenrechte—Heuchelei und Wahrheit." *Einheit* 32, no. 9 (September 1977): 1036–44.

Kramer, Andrew E. "Lyudmila Alexeyeva, 'Grandmother' of Russia's Human Rights Movement, Dies at 91." *New York Times*, December 9, 2018.

Kuper, Simon. "The Resonance of Andrei Sakharov in Putin's Russia." *Financial Times*, December 31, 2021.

Minnerup, Gunter. "East Germany's Frozen Revolution." *New Left Review* 132 (March–April 1982).

Nacken, Angela. "Immer Mehr wagen den Kampf mit den DDR-Behörden." *Frankfurter Allgemeine Zeitung*, August 21, 1976.

Osnos, Peter. "Accumulating Irritants Peril Détente; Soviet Mood Sullen for Geneva Talks." *Washington Post*, May 18, 1977.

———. "European Security Charter Bogged Down in Difficulties." *Washington Post*, June 22, 1974.

———. "Helsinki Process Outlives Détente's Demise." *Washington Post*, September 12, 1983.

———. "President Leonid Ilyich Brezhnev: 1906–1982; The Apparatchik Who Led the Soviet Board of Directors." *Washington Post*, November 12, 1982.

"Repräsentanten von 35 Staaten signierten die Schlußakte der Konferenz von Helsinki." *Neues Deutschland* (East Berlin), August 2–3, 1975.

Reston, James. "Letter from Belgrade." *New York Times*, March 1, 1978.

Russell, Harold. "The Helsinki Declaration: Brobdingnag or Lilliput," *American Journal of International Law* 70 (April 1976).

Sarotte, M. E. "The Betrayal Myth Behind Putin's Brinksmanship." *Wall Street Journal*, January 8–9, 2022.

Schudel, Matt. "George S. Vest, Long-Serving Foreign Service Officer, and Cold War Diplomat, Dies at 102." *Washington Post*, August 26, 2021.

Shafir, Michael. "Who Is Paul Goma?" *Index on Censorship* 7, no. 1 (1978).

Shcharansky, Anatoly, Yelena Bonner, and Lyudmila Alexeyeva. "The Tenth Year of the Watch." *New York Review of Books*, June 26, 1986.

Sherer, Albert W. Jr. "Helsinki's Child: Goldberg's Variation." *Foreign Policy* 39 (Summer 1980): 154–59.

Skilling, H. Gordon. "Czechoslovakia and Helsinki." *Canadian Slavonic Papers* 18, no. 3 (September 1976): 245–65.

Slezkine, Peter. "From Helsinki to Human Rights Watch: How an American Cold War Monitoring Group Became an International Human Rights Institution." *Humanity* (Winter 2014): 345–70.

Snyder, Sarah B. "'Jerry, Don't Go': Domestic Opposition to the 1975 Helsinki Final Act." *Journal of American Studies* 44, no. 1 (February 2010): 67–81.

"Two Hundred Days Since Helsinki." *Horizont* (East Berlin) from JPRS, Translations 67151 (April 16, 1976): 1–9.

Varadarajan, Tunku. "The Two Blunders That Caused the Ukraine War." *Wall Street Journal*, March 5–6, 2022.

Walker, Barbara. "The Moscow Correspondents, Soviet Human Rights Activists, and the Problem of the Western Gift." In Choi Chatterjee and Beth Holmgren, eds. *Americans Experience Russia: Encountering the Enigma, 1917 to the Present.* New York: Routledge, 2013.

Reports

Commission on Security and Cooperation. "The Belgrade Followup Meeting to the Conference of Security and Cooperation in Europe: A Report and Appraisal," May 17, 1978.

European Parliament. "The Organization for Security and Co-Operation in Europe (OSCE): A Pillar of the European Security Order," 2021.

The Final Act. Helsinki, August 1, 1975.

Human Rights Watch. *World Report/2020.* New York: Seven Stories Press, 2020.

Nóvé, Béla. "The Documents of Cultural Forum and Counter-Forum Budapest 1985." *COURAGE Registry*, 2019, http://cultural-opposition.eu/registry/?uri=http://courage.btk.mta.hu/courage/individual/n3110.

OSCE. "Report on Violations of International Humanitarian and Human Rights Law, War Crimes and Crimes against Humanity," April 12, 2022.

Ostoja-Ostaszewski, A. et al., eds. *Dissent in Poland, Reports, and Documents Dec. 1975–July 1977.* London: Association of Polish Students and Graduates in Exile, 1977.

Petrescu, Cristina. "Paul Goma Private Archive." *COURAGE Registry*, 2019, http://cultural-opposition.eu/registry/?uri=http://courage.btk.mta.hu/courage/individual/n158100.

Precan, Vile, ed. *Human Rights in Czechoslovakia: A Documentation, September 1981–December 1982.* Paris: International Committee for the Support of Charter 77 in Czechoslovakia, April 1983.

Radio Free Europe. "Six Months After: The East European Response to Helsinki." *Radio Free Europe Background Report* 46, February 18, 1976.

Schöpflin, George. *Witness to Cultural Genocide: First-Hand Reports on Rumania's Minority Policies Today.* New York: American Transylvanian Federation, January 1, 1979.

Snyder, Sarah B. "Symbolic Politics and the Cold War: How Helsinki Watch Personalized Human Rights Abuses." Presentation at the Rapoport Center for Human Rights and Justice at the University of Texas, September 14, 2009.

U.S. Commission on Security and Cooperation in Europe, *Basket Three: Implementation of the Helsinki Accords*, Vol. 2, Hearings. Washington, DC: Government Printing Office, 1977.

———. *The Belgrade Follow-up Meeting to the Conference on Security and Cooperation in Europe: A Report and Appraisal.* Washington, DC: Government Printing Office, 1978.

———. *The Crisis in Poland and Its Effects on the Helsinki Process*, Hearings. Washington, DC: Government Printing Office, December 28, 1981.

———. *The Madrid CSCE Review Conference*, November 1983.

———. *The Right to Know, the Right to Act: Documents of Helsinki Dissent from the Soviet Union and Eastern Europe.* Washington, DC: May 1978.

Acknowledgments

Peter L. W. Osnos

In a way, work on this book began in 1974 when the *Washington Post* sent me to the Soviet Union as its correspondent. I wrote about the negotiations for what became the Helsinki Accords in 1975.

My father-in-law, Ambassador Albert W. Sherer Jr., was head of the US delegation, and his brother-in-law Harold S. Russell was the legal adviser from the State Department. This coincidence of roles and its personal dimension have continued over the decades, both on the issues in the accords and the development of Human Rights Watch as the leading global monitoring group.

I have been at various times a reporter, supporter, board member, and occasional critic of HRW. This book is an amalgam of those experiences.

The list of those who contributed to my account in this narrative includes dissidents, activists, historians, politicians, diplomats, journalists, and the extraordinary staff at Helsinki Watch and later Human Rights Watch.

In particular, Robert L. Bernstein, Jeri Laber, and Aryeh Neier were core founders of the organization and largely devised the investigatory and advocacy approach of its strategy. The only surviving member of the original Helsinki monitoring group in Moscow is Natan Sharansky. We have been, as he describes us, "collaborators" for almost fifty years.

Holly Cartner, the quintessence of a human rights professional, was the perfect choice to enhance this book with her expertise.

The book's editor is Paul Golob, master of the craft and as always invaluable. Christine Marra is the managing editor of Platform Books and enables a complicated process to succeed. Malka Margolies is the determined publicist. Alex Baker is the gifted designer of the dust jacket. And the team at Two Rivers/Ingram brings the book to booksellers and therefore to readers.

Susan Sherer Osnos has been with me on this project from the outset, and its results are as much hers as they are mine, except for its flaws.

Holly Cartner

A special word of gratitude goes to Jeri Laber, the former executive director of Helsinki Watch, and Aryeh Neier, the former executive director of Human Rights Watch, who were particularly generous with their time and willing to share their memories of the early years of the organization. A number of other former and current Human Rights Watch staff and board members also took time to speak with me about Helsinki Watch, including Holly Burkhalter, Cathy Fitzpatrick, Janet Fleischman, Bruce Rabb, and Joanna Weschler, whose insights contributed greatly to this project. I am very grateful to Fred Abrahams, who reviewed the discussion of HRW's work on Kosovo while on sabbatical.

I consulted with Vera Cîmpeanu regarding key details related to my work in Romania. She was at that time, and remains today, a very special friend. I am also indebted to Jane Day, a friend and professional librarian at Duke University, who voluntarily tracked down many documents in multiple languages.

I would like to express my sincere appreciation to Peter and Susan Osnos for their wisdom, patience, and encouragement throughout this project. I learned a lot from working with them.

Finally, I would like to thank my family—Uli, Sophie, and Dylan Schempp—for their support: Everything in life is just a lot better when they are around, and I love them dearly.

Index

About the Authors

PETER L. W. OSNOS is the author of *An Especially Good View: Watching History Happen* and the editor of *George Soros: A Life in Full.* He is the founder of the publishing house PublicAffairs and a former publisher of the Times Books imprint at Random House, where he was previously a senior editor and associate publisher. Prior to his career in book publishing, he spent eighteen years at the *Washington Post,* where he was a correspondent in Saigon, Moscow, and London and served as foreign editor and national editor. He is a graduate of Brandeis University and the Columbia School of Journalism, and his writing has appeared in the *Atlantic, Foreign Affairs,* and *Columbia Journalism Review,* among other publications. He lives in New York City.

HOLLY CARTNER is a human rights lawyer who has been active in the field for more than thirty years. As the executive director of the Europe and Central Asia division of Human Rights Watch, as Helsinki Watch is now known, she oversaw research and advocacy work, conducted briefings and advocacy with high-level government officials, and supervised staff based in the United States and throughout the region. She previously established and headed a field office for Human Rights Watch in Romania and conducted research, reporting, and advocacy on human rights abuses, in particular on the Roma minority and on right-wing violence in Germany following reunification. She also served on the executive committee of the International Helsinki Federation. Since leaving Human Rights Watch in 2010, she has worked as an independent consultant for human rights and philanthropic institutions and nongovernmental organizations. She lives in Chapel Hill, North Carolina.

PLATFORM

New York

For information about this and other books from
Platform Books visit platformbooksllc.net.